OLD RECTORY
or The Interview

OLD RECTORY
or The Interview

___

MARTYN SKINNER

The past never leaves us,
and the future is already here.

LEWIS MUMFORD

MICHAEL RUSSELL

First published by the Rampant Lions Press
12 Chesterton Road, Cambridge

© Martyn Skinner 1970, 1973, 1977

This edition published 1984
by Michael Russell (Publishing) Ltd
The Chantry, Wilton, Salisbury, Wiltshire

Printed by Blackmore Press,
Shaftesbury, Dorset

To
HUGH WATERMAN
and
BEDE GRIFFITHS
formerly of Eastington

PROLOGUE
in Two Concurrent Scenes

SCENE I

*The scene opens in the garden of an English village
inn, overlooking a remote and depopulated countryside.
The time, in the early years of the post-plague era. Dic
Fossick, a professional interviewer, is having a drink and
discussion with two of his friends, Baytre and J.J.Ponder.
They are on their way to interview a local hermit or
solitary, about whom Fossick has already made some
preliminary enquiries. Accompanied by Baytre, he has
just returned from a tour of similar interviews in Europe,
and they have asked Ponder to join them for the last
assignment in the series.*

FOSSICK

His name? Why need a hermit have a name?
Old Rectory is what he's called round here –
That is, by those who call him anything.
They know the house exists because up there
Beside the church, above that woody swaddle
Of shrubs and conifers, a chimney pokes.
They know the man exists, because it smokes.

PONDER

He's never seen outside?

FOSSICK   Never by day;
And rarely as a badger in the lanes
By night. It's then he fetches up supplies,
And sometimes a latecomer for a pint
Will sight and shun him, taking a long cut
– He startles them – and, greeted at the bar,
Drink out on it: 'I met Old Rectory'

PONDER
He has no callers?

FOSSICK   Callers? Who but us?
They say the postman hasn't called for years.

PONDER
He's lived here long?

FOSSICK   Since just before the plague.

PONDER
Well, what a comment on our post-plague era!
Odd solitaries could exist before:
Clerical Crusoes, spinsters mewed with cats –
But anonymity – to need no name
For tax return or rate demand or census
Or register of government electors!
– What a reversion! It's as if we'd dreamed
The last progressive century or two;
And waking up, discovered they weren't true.

FOSSICK
Yes, a world-setback was the Porton Sneeze.
The mucus sprayed by that micrologist
Who'd bred a virus which no viricide
Could cope with – rabbits, oddly, were immune –
Meant more than just a thousand million deaths.
It meant what we have come to call abeyance:
Civilization, progress in abeyance;
A halt in history, almost a hiatus
In which we huddle now. Who could have guessed?

BAYTRE
Not those who plotted population charts,
Before the plague assuring us that soon
We should be shitting on each other's shoulders –

Instead, round here one hardly needs a hedge.

PONDER
Well, weren't we warned by scientists that knew?

BAYTRE
While from the rest we learned what the pooh-pooh
Of Noah's neighbours must have sounded like!

PONDER
Yet if the prospect sometimes made us shudder,
How different is the shudder that we give
In retrospect – the residue who live –
When we remember what the plague was like:
In city streets the only sign of life
Disposal of the dead; and only then
At scheduled times, when the hearse-unit plied
From house to house, and with hydraulic grab
Picked up and piled into its gruesome bin
Corpses put out like refuse at the kerb.

FOSSICK
If you must shudder, why not here – and now?
To some extent at least we've normalized
Our urban – even our conurban – life.
Back in the future, men forget the past.
Out here the past's still present. Farmers here
Are fewer than the farms. Blanks, county-wide,
Of idle roads, deserted villages,
Oasis pubs . . .

BAYTRE   Or else as when we saw
Across a tumble-treed and ungrazed park
That open, empty mansion, its sole life
The blue pause of a peacock in a porch
Back to the terrace trailing from indoors.

FOSSICK

If even before the plague the hermit urge
Was gaining strength, as restlessness for rest
And craving after quiet made men long
To opt, drop out, civilization-sick,
Their only bar, a want of wilderness,
What marvel was it if the movement spread,
When all at once the wilderness was there;
When even what were known as the Home Counties
Became a desolation overnight:
Surrey, available for solitude;
Sussex, a ready-made Stylites-land
As hermit-worthy as a Flemish landscape?
For though they feared infection, and so shunned
Void houses like – I almost said the plague –
Barns, disused churches, signal-boxes, sheds
There were in plenty for them to convert,
Without requiring – such were in abeyance –
Estate agent's appointment to inspect,
Or architect to furnish detailed plans,
Or planning body (death is no respecter
Of quorums) to consider and consent.

BAYTRE

As hermit-worthy as a Flemish landscape.
Jerome in Sussex! It reminds us well
That Europe had its hermits once before;
Reminds us, too, that we're familiar
With what they looked like, crouched in cave or cell,
And walling some great Gallery, Beaux-Arts,
Brussels or Ghent, where Memlinc, Van der Goes,
Bosch, Patinir, or even perhaps (who knows?)
Some Master of the Hermits, fixed in paint

4

Their postures of temptation or repose;
The landscape-theme, the variation-saint.
Did they, those artists in their studios
Among the stepped-up gables, spires and towers,
Regard their hermits much as we do ours:
Fugitives from satiety, who longed
To opt, drop out, civilization-sick,
And disengage from Rome, which even then
Was million-peopled, and the world's Great Wen,
Or worse, its Bubo?

PONDER   Bubo! Don't you, Dic,
Agree with me that Rome perhaps was wronged?
Permissive, yes – but was it so depraved?
Its hermits fled because they would be saved.

BAYTRE
Yes, from its sex-pit – saved from its *corruptio*
Optimi pessima – the hardened heart
In the softened body, flabby-violent.
If you would judge the depth of its descent
Into that pit, and height from which it fell,
A double list of names and nouns will tell –
Regulus, Cato, Scipio, Lucretia –
Such were the types of earlier fame. Of later,
Some famous strumpet's favourite gladiator:
Or the imperial *voyeur*, in his isle's
Seclusion (and the sense faints picturing
Its azure sweetness) organizing orgies,
Watching his *Spintriae* defiled in files,
Tiberius, his *mentula* at milk,
Infansturbatio; or Messalina,
Stealing, gilt-dugged, from her imperial bed,
Vulvae tentigine, to prey on garbage.

5

Next take the nouns – say, *gravitas, decorum,*
Pietas, virtus, jus, respublica :
Word-monuments in Rome's vocabulary
To what Rome stood for once. So turn the page
To the latter lexicon: *luxuria,*
Thermae, circenses, tribas, cinaedus,
Fellator, irrumatio, cunnilingus . . .

PONDER

At least we learn that Martial and Petronius
Used terms – how unlike ours – that were euphonious,
And so could be mellifluously lewd.
But let's get back to Jerome. I've been wanting
To ask you, since *he* can't be interviewed,
What reasons gave the Jeromes *de nos jours*
Whom you *have* interviewed, for their absconding?
What sort of men, too, were these modern Stylites?
I've come in at the tail-end of your tour,
And should, before we make this final call,
Enjoy a brief description of them all –
Not all, that is – just one or two, the highlights.

BAYTRE

It is the hermitages I recall
More than the hermits. Highlights? There were two:
Both sets of buildings – one in Portugal,
One England – long disused, and in their functions
As diverse as a piston and a pew;
And yet alike in this, that each resembled
One of those void, eviscerated shells
Which with its whorls intact, is taken over
And lived in by a crab – a hermit crab.
The one was on a cape where Europe ended
In hills remoter than horizon-clouds,

6

Matching in solitude the mid-Atlantic;
Its only life just sea-birds, and one man;
For many years just sea-birds. And the man –
It was a shock to come across him there
Not in turf shed or beehive hut, but crossing
What seemed a derelict church-sided square
In isolation, isolation made
Intenser by no vestige of a town.
It was a pilgrim church – a famous shrine –
The square, a square-wide street of pilgrim cells
Like almshouses, where once perhaps some good
Wyf of bisydë Sevill might have lodged;
But now its long arcaded symmetry
Gap-roofed, with slides of tumbled tiles in front
Greying the grassiness which, near the church,
Was by a set of footpaths vaguely tracked,
Converging on the last lodge still intact;
And here . . .

PONDER   You found your subject for research.
Tell me of him – the inmate, not the square.
What did *he* look like?

BAYTRE   If you want the faces,
They're Dic's concern. My *forte* is the places.
And since, as I have said, these make a pair,
You'll have to have them both. A Devon lane
Humped by a bridge of brick led to the other:
A railway bridge, but what was left to tell
That once it had been blackened by the smoke
Its small arch used to intercept and smother,
Swirling from this, then that side as the train
Chugged through the cutting – now a weedy choke:

7

Its cleft once functional and regular
A wilderness of may and dog-rose shell
Embellishing the landscape with its scar;
The permanent way become a permanent dell.
Yes, what was left to tell,
Until we turned and saw the signal-box
Like a gazebo at the platform end,
A rim of platform lost in grass and docks,
And taller weeds, gold fennel and thin bent
That on the funnelled breezes seemed to float,
As if from crack or fissure there had cropped
A wildflower-border in the station stone?
And where the trains once stopped
Between the platforms blazed a poppy moat.
And where the porter gardened between trains
Red floribundas into thickets grown;
Cow parsley and a pergola's remains;
In bracken a sidalcea alone.
And as we strolled or stood,
We noticed one fire-bucket, like a toy,
Scarlet behind some fireweed massed in bud;
A rusty buffer wreathed in traveller's joy;
An ivied lamp post – underneath its hood
We crunched on broken glass as we walked by.
And round the platform awning, creeper-clad
And rickety, serrating the blue sky
That wooden, pointed pelmet stations had.
Birds sang as if it had been Adelstrop.
For Nature . . .

   FOSSICK   Bay, you're starting to digress.
It's time for us to start, and you to stop.

PONDER
But you did find your hermit?

BAYTRE   Him? O yes.
He'd seen us gazing down the cutting-coombe.
And slipped into his cell, the waiting-room.

PONDER
And there?

FOSSICK Come on, you'll get no more from Bay.
At least you'll meet Old Rectory. On our way
I'll quench your queries – that is, if you're quick.

PONDER
Well, first of all . . .

FOSSICK   Here, Bay you've left your stick.
Sorry, J. J. . . .

PONDER   . . . I wanted to discuss
What impulse prompted this mass exodus.
Those earlier anchorites, Rome's, Antioch's
Were all religious, Christian, orthodox;
And shared a common dread – contamination;
A common purpose – prayer and meditation.
But these you've interviewed, these hermit crabs
Squatted round Europe in their strange post-fabs,
Did you observe in these a common bond
That made them, as I asked before, abscond?
A shared aversion, single hope in view
That drove them out in to the wilds or drew?
Civilization-sick? – the term's too vague.
Weren't many merely scuttling from the plague?

FOSSICK
A few: but that would hardly make them stay,

9

The plague being past. Civilization-sick?
Some hold that human psyches are like leaves,
And as the *zeitgeist* rustles, fluctuate
Collectively, unconscious they're connected.
But if some conscious sickness did exist,
(Some kind of metropoliphobia)
Its victims varied. Every interview
Disclosed a different symptom of disgust –
Disgust grown up through years before the plague
Transformed the things they fled from, as they fled.
One saw his Limbo as two windowed stacks,
Night-flat, day-office, rush-hour multitudes
Ferried between them through a Stygian tube.
What most weighed down another was the city's
Interminable spread: shops, houses, shops,
Shops, houses, shops, repetitive as waves
Of a vast built-up sea, shops, houses, shops.
It was the citizens and not the city
Depressed a third: what he called Mammon's mob,
The multi-craving monster with its mass
Manipulated addict-appetite.
One, like a rogue ant from a termitary,
Fled from autocracy by automation;
One from its opposite – both co-existed:
In office the computer, round the flat
The neo-anarchy of gang-prowled streets,
And protest rioter and lout at large.
Several (and here at least they were agreed)
Were fugitives from sex, promiscuous
Obsessive sex, with all taboos taboo.
With what engrossed repugnance they discussed
The sex-pit they'd escaped from – if they had

(Escaped its facts but not its fantasies):
Al fresco mating in the public parks,
Or simulated on the public stage
To give a phallic fillip to a play.
The female form, the great all-advertiser,
Provocative on posters; and no less
Provocative in skirts like pelvic pelmets,
Accentuating what they hardly hid.
Bookshops like pornemporia, titles stocked
Which even bishops couldn't recommend,
Or open-minded and close-conscienced dons
Who saw the funny side of Fanny Sade . . .

    PONDER
I hesitate to interrupt you, Dic,
But it was *your* proviso, 'If you're quick.'
So far you've hardly given me a chance
To show I can be. As I've kept my glance
Fixed on that – what was it you called them, those
Trees up there round the Rectory, now quite close,
That woody swaddle, was it? – I'm aware
That we shall reach it, if I don't take care,
Before we've left the sex-pit.
                      Now, Dic, these
Cases you've mentioned, weren't they refugees
Rather than true recluses; more, let's say,
Driven by fear or hate to break away
Than drawn by hope of some new life ahead
To seek a haven where it might be led,
Some Patmos, Grasmere even?

    FOSSICK   Partly, yes.
From-ites and to-ites, all were more or less.
But they could be distinguished, yes that's true,

As could the to-ites from each other, too.
There were the natural hermits, solitaries
Who next to their own company, preferred
That of the sea or hills or clouds or sheep.
The Simple Lifers, water from a well,
Warmth from a wood, a garden and a goat.
The transcendental sector: mystic tramps,
Self-gurus, sufis, zen-men searching out
The Buddha-womb or the Eternal Suchness.
    PONDER
No Christians?

    FOSSICK   Genuine Jeromes? One or two.
The strangest cult the nature-devotees,
Wordsworthiani et hoc omne genus,
Who dispossessed by tourism and traffic,
Now streamed back to the stricken countryside
Like zealots to a liberated shrine.
Why, there was one – Bay, here, will bear me out –
Who when we primed him with our leading question
('What was it prompted you?' etcetera)
Beckoned us out (it was an evening session)
To view a spread of moonlit scenery
Without one living twinkle near or far,
From street or window in its solitude.
' "How sweet the moonlight sleeps upon this bank" –
That was what prompted me,' was all he said.
But added, as our parley moved indoors,
That, living in a town, for him the moon
Had been in exile to electric light:
Diminished, disregarded, dimmed, eclipsed
By neon dazzle, a forgotten disc.
Then, scuttling from infection, one broad night,

Entranced, he saw it re-enact that line
Of treasured poetry upon a patch
Of rough grass by a solitary shack.
No alien light intruded – so he stayed.
Sheer lunacy – for once the platitude
Is justified.

PONDER He wasn't on a trip?

FOSSICK
No: drugs, like better things, were in abeyance.
Besides, the hermit's was too strenuous
A life for drop-outs; they dropped in again,
And joined communities

PONDER   Communities?
Were such included in your series?

FOSSICK   No.
We hope to do them in a separate tour.
By all accounts, their cranks and oddities
Will make our hermits seem a pod of peas.

PONDER
Hardly: your catalogue appears to range
From spinach to asparagus. It's strange,
However, that you can't suggest some hall-
Or hermit-mark to designate them all;
Some shared or common factor.

FOSSICK   Well, I can:
Fantasy. All were fugitives, who ran
Not from the plague but fact; who fled to seek
A refuge, not exactly in *mystique*
But fantasies more suited to the mood
Of, let's say, amateurs of solitude:

13

Fasts, nature-raptures, visionary trips,
Prophetic broodings, penances with whips
After some devils' . . . tempt-in should I call
It nowadays? What use, what point is all
Such non-activity and abstinence?
Will flagellation help repair that fence,
For instance – reveries re-hang that gate?

BAYTRE
Best ask Old Rectory – it's his estate.

FOSSICK
What! . . . why, you're right. That comes of too
    much talk
– It takes all sense of distance from a walk.
At least we've no appointment, so there's time
To find our bearings.

PONDER   Phew! It's quite a climb.
They loved to perch, these later rectories:
Unlike the Georgian.

BAYTRE   This fringe of trees
(Some rector must have avenued the lane
As if he saw it as his private drive)
Should intercept the weather when it's rough,
And help to shield the house.

FOSSICK   It's close enough.
I'd thought of it as further back than this:
Not just a lawn's length – if that was a lawn –
In from the gate . . .

PONDER   If that is still a gate.
THE – look – OLD RECTORY: Some wag has scored
A W, and arrowed in a K.

14

BAYTRE

Yet we were right to call it an estate:
House, garden, glebe; all things in order stored.
And still, in spite of long neglect and gaps
And overgrowth, what once it was is plain.
D'you see beyond that yew shun, half-way up,
How the old walled-in kitchen-garden traps
Sun for an early acre with its cup.
Or, higher still, that curious terrace-ledge –
What d'you think went on behind its hedge?
A bowling-green? An alcoved belvedere
With Venus-ended vista?

PONDER   Hardly here.

BAYTRE

I wonder what we'd find if we walked round?·
An ice-house – subterranean cabinet
With ferny steps and door into a mound?
Or home-built druid circle, garden size?
Or brambled monument (some household pet)?
Or vestige more pathetic: sunken nook
Like a small quarry, where the garden's brook
Had been diverted to divert a child,
Cherished and delicate and doomed; its glade
Still traceable, with mimic cliffs that rise
A sapling's height, and lakelet and cascade
And tiny alpine cottage gone to wild?
No less the garden down here by the gate
Evokes that rectory life so long gone by.
Soft sunshine on the February oaks
Above the crocuses. Or in July,
Heard from the lane, staccato yet sedate,

15

The clonk of mallets, and between the strokes
Gay laughter at the local Kilvert's jokes.
And now the grass they played on is hoop-high.
Perhaps the last incumbent let it grow.
Bachelor, bookworm – can't you see him so? –
He ran things in a sedentary way,
And hated change: his foible to prefer
Nature to make it, if it must occur,
Rather than man – so let the place decay
And hardly noticed change that was so slow.
Easy enough to visualize it all:
Nothing kept up, or under, or replaced.
Elder or guelder-rose in gapes of wall.
Even the pointed, gothic garden door
Which gave him private access to the waste
Of churchyard hay he waded through to church,
No longer on the latch but on the lurch.
One hedge alone perhaps he clipped with care,
Which might have dwindled otherwise the view
He loved to muse on from his terrace shelf.
But look! There's someone moving . . .

PONDER   Someone? Who?

BAYTRE

Look! On that very terrace! There – up there!
Great Betch! It's him, Old Rectory himself.

Gesticulates, pointing excitedly

FOSSICK

No need to wave – he will have seen us, too –
Or if he hasn't, and the chatter's right,
Will have foreseen us.

PONDER   You mean second-sight?

FOSSICK

I mean that is what they believe round here.
The Evil Eye could hardly cause more fear.
We know – as you, J. J., must know as well –
That since the plague the old beliefs in spell,
Witch, wizardry have tended to revive.
In parts like this they're very much alive.
And so our friend here, who may well possess
Some psychic power – hypnosis, at a guess –
Has come to be a kind of local boast
Or legend, half believed-in, like a ghost,
Half dreaded, like a species – yes it's true –
Of Faust with whom the devil's hoof-in-shoe.
Some vow – you know what village rumours are –
A poltergeist is his familiar.
A sorcerer in drugs, claims one report,
Of a traumatic, soul-transporting sort.
Has fresco'd half the church, another says,
(With art as apposite to such a place
As Gauguin's in San Marco, we'll suppose,
Or in Tahiti Fra Angelico's).
We can expect, if all is true they tell,
An Admirable Crichton of the cell.

PONDER

Yet still a fantasist?

FOSSICK   He's bound to be.

PONDER

You likened him to Faust.

FOSSICK   Yes, I agree,
The similarity is not exact.
Since, though for years, assisted by his pact,

Faust set himself to lead, like some recluse,
A life of aspiration, not of use,
In the last act he found the saving clue:
And unlike him we're going to interview
Who lives aloof from facts as well as men,
Forsook his fantasies – and drained a fen.

SCENE II

*Shortly before the arrival of his interviewers Old
Rectory is sitting out of sight at the shady end of his
terrace – once a hilltop bowling green devised by an
eccentric rector – indulging in a soliloquy to the clouds.
He then reflects on the point and purpose of his hermit
life, and his premonition that he will one day be visited.
It is at this point that his callers reveal their presence;
he moves forward, and in turn reveals his own.*

So easily it might have been one day
Of weekly drench, the other six blank blue:
A system suited to a Darwin world
Where function is the *modus evolvendi*.
Instead, the heavenly hose – as men once drank
Their tea from whorls of Worcester, and their wine
From goblets of superfluous perfection –
Involves the sky's great gallery of clouds
In all its contrast and variety
Of theme and treatment; nimbus, cumulus
And cirrus: windy mare's tails, mack'relings
Of mottled pearl, beards, bolsters, arabesques,
Acropolises, awnings, anvils, alps;

May-billows so celestially white
One looks for Juno's peacock; drizzle-grey
Hill-hackles; clouds that pageant the horizon
Or pile up in stupendous aggregates
Above what seems to be a map-sized earth,
Then fade away to leave the fading sky
At planet-time with one flamingo wisp –
Here, on my terrace, can I catalogue
This sky-collection as it circulates
Its weather-portraits, studies in set fair;
Or frescoes of the winds, each with its own
Distinctive cloudscape: from the clear north-west
Sharp diamond light undistancing the hills,
And blurs like quarry dust of weltering hail –
How different when beyond old Dunkery
Rain musters, and the various-clouded rack
Streams inland till the white, invaded sky
Seems on the move with a horizon-host.
Lucky I am to have this perfect perch
Where any time of day, and any number
Of times a day, I can mooch out unmet,
And watch unwatched and pry in privacy;
Then back into the church, my studio,
Or else my study, down there in the house,
To add to my own frescoes, or to brood
On God, death, doom beyond the outer sky;
Dreams, urges, guilts beneath the inner one:
The cosmos that's within us. Beckoned here
By nature's wilderness I fled from man's
To ponder, even perhaps to paint my way
Back to reality. Reality –
Back there confined to and confused with facts

The brain can check or senses certify:
Bricks, bissels, tissue on a boxer's scar,
Cash, cybernetics, cancer, $2\pi r$,
Skin pigment, sewage system, stock and share,
Cubic capacity or pubic hair –
Hard facts, yet from them what soft fantasies
Luxuriate, hopes, yearnings, cravings sprung
From groins and gadgets, gambling, games and goods:
Beach reveries – enticed by lounging limbs
The mind at dalliance while the body basks;
Arena frenzies, round a booted ball
The static host of yell-participants;
Lottery longings, a pool's paradise;
Board-room cigar-dreams, piling London up
Into a Mammonstrosity; millenial
Schemings to mould and marshall the unborn
In U, New, Ultra, Super topias –
Delusions all, resulting in an era
Cocksure, cockeyed, cock-happy – not for me,
Who took to flight when even before the plague
Civilization was called so-called,
An early solitary: others followed
In spiritual seepage – so again
As history half repeats itself, we find
Rome at the rim and hermits at the hub.
What point the hub, though, if no spokes connect?
Unviewed my paintings, ponderings unheeded
Except by neighbour hermits when we meet
Nocturnally, and pay each other visits
Unknown to local knowalls. Local knowalls!
They think I've second sight – foresee what's going
To happen here, where nothing ever does.

Nothing? I have a hunch that something will;
A premonition, recently grown stronger,
That one day, strangers, callers, will intrude;
Birds that will peck my seed up, fly away
And like involuntary colporteurs
Transplant it – visitors from inner space –
Men Friday – strange presentiment . . .
                                        Great Scott!
Look, down there, something moving – by the gate –
Three figures – human figures – and by day!
They must be strangers – callers! It's as if
My thoughts had fetched them here. But that would be
Telekinesis not telepathy,
And they are men, not dice. What Jung would call
Meaningful synchronicity perhaps.
What panic once they would have put me in
And sent me into hiding for a week.
But now they're welcome – spokes to serve my turn –
Intruders I'll inoculate with truth,
The desert serum. So, they've seen me too,
And wave me down, as for an interview.
An interview? If that's what they're about,
With some imagined recluse, crazed and dumb,
Perhaps, they'll wonder, when I let them out,
Whether, if they had guessed, they would have come.

*He signals back, and leaves the terrace. After a short
discussion the three friends saunter up to meet him, and
disappear behind the yew shun that screens the walled
kitchen garden from the house.*

THE SESSION
in Seven Scenes

SCENE I

OLD RECTORY *and his three interviewers, having met somewhere in the higher levels of the garden, descend to the house together ; they pause in a little group between the great yew hedge and the front door, while they discuss a preliminary problem : what the hermit is to be called.*

OLD RECTORY
My surname, gentlemen, what's that to you?
A hermit, like a rose, by any name . . .
Even a nickname, like Old Rectory. Why
Drag in my surname?

FOSSICK   For an interview
Such local appellations will not do.
We need a name we can address you by.

OLD RECTORY
You'd like to call me Mr So and So.

FOSSICK
We'll call you – rector. That you're not ordained
Can, when we introduce you, be explained.
The church is, after all, your studio.

OLD RECTORY
Tell me, these others whom you've interviewed –
Did they all furnish names?

FOSSICK   No, there were some
Failed even that – all similarly dumb
In different languages. Long solitude
Had left them obmutescent, quite untuned

25

Their vocal chords, like castaways marooned
On desert islands.

BAYTRE   Hardly similar;
In some sense hardly dumb. One gave a croak
Of greeting, raucous as a raven; one
Had in his throat a cellar-door ajar
On rusty hinges; one an ivy-screech
On gusty windows; when another spoke,
We heard a shoulder-parrot – or Ben Gunn.

PONDER
Yet you, the doyen of the desert, speak
Without the least suspicion of a creak,
Or hitch or haver. To have kept its tone
Your larynx must have been in constant use.
Perhaps you read aloud – or even preach?

OLD RECTORY
What, to an empty church of easel-pews?
My voice gets used, like yours, in normal speech.

PONDER
Speech – why, with whom?

OLD RECTORY   My visitors.

FOSSICK   Your what?
They said the postman hadn't called for years,
And that our visit here would be unique.

OLD RECTORY
Well, so it may be. Bless their eyes and ears!
They think I'm always resident – I'm not –
See no one – when it's an unusual week
That doesn't bring some contact with our clique . . .

PONDER
Clique! – out here in this next to nowhere spot?

OLD RECTORY
It's small, of course, a four-man coterie
Of neighbour hermits who have settled near:
Ralph Brompton Ralph, Dirk Willett, Malachi
Monksilver, and myself Old Rectory here.
As for our expeditions out of doors,
We use late darkness when all gossip snores,
And badger-like noctambulating by,
Drop in for pot-luck and a colloquy.
To-night – who knows? one, several may appear.

FOSSICK
More reason to speed up our interview.
Bay, the recorders: to withdraw with you
[*addressing* OLD RECTORY]
(As Hamlet said) – I'd like to get things placed,
Seating, and so forth.

OLD RECTORY   Sure, but why the haste?
Need we complete this session in a day,
To-morrow's being at night?

FOSSICK   What's that you say?
To-morrow's session.

OLD RECTORY   Yes, there will be two.
You fossick me, I torquemada you.
Up at the church you'll need one night at least
For catechism – though I'm not its priest.
Come in, come in – through here – I'll lead the way.

PONDER [*pausing, and lowering his voice*]
Is this in order?

FOSSICK   Don't fuss – once we're through
With session one, we'll scarper; till we are
Best go along with him – it won't be far.

PONDER
It's a tough morsel that your interview
Has bitten off.

FOSSICK
                No more than we can chew.
[*raising his voice*]
We're coming, rector. J.J., after you.

They go in. Baytre, having fetched the apparatus,
follows.

SCENE II

*When the scene opens, the living room of the Old
Rectory appears to be occupied by three recumbent
and immobilized forms, those of the three interviewers.
The room is large enough to take more than one sofa as
well as several armchairs; and in the centre is a table
with chairs round it pushed back as if recently vacated;
on it is an oblong, plastic box. The voice of its owner
can be heard in the hall as he welcomes two of his
hermit neighbours,* DIRK WILLETT *and* RALPH
BROMPTON RALPH, *and ushers them in to share the
shock of his surprise visitors.*

OLD RECTORY
I hoped you'd come if I hoped hard enough.
Telesperance – or what's the Greek for hope?
Come in, come in: you'll never guess – don't try –
Just what it is – but 'what's' an unfair clue –
Since what it is I've hoped you round to meet
Isn't just what at all – you well may stare –
But even more incredibly, just who.

DIRK and RALPH
Who?

OLD RECTORY
        Who: there, there and there.
[*entering and pointing at the three forms*]
It's not their fault they look the worse for dope,
And seem to want to shake hands with their feet.

29

RALPH
Who are they?

OLD RECTORY Hermit-fanciers, on beat
Round Europe – how they'd relish Malachi,
Our picture Jerome with his great white ruff
Of beard, and naked torso, summer-buff;
And what a prize your turreted retreat
Catching the eye on Willett, Dirk, would be:
The only Folly in their inventory
Of hermitages.

DIRK   Well, they picked on you.
What happened – did you grant an interview?

OLD RECTORY
Yes, I've been under the Stylitescope.

RALPH
Already?

OLD RECTORY We've held session number one.
The second, in the church to-morrow night
Is my addition, which our little group
Considering superfluous, had planned
To cut and run from – scarper was the word –
(Hyperaesthesia: I overheard)
And since I think the fixture ought to stand,
Here they still are.

DIRK   And we have missed the fun . . .

OLD RECTORY
Of their being dormitived?

DIRK   No, no, of your
Being psychoviewed. Well, if it's done, it's done.

30

But how I wish there could be an encore
With us as audience.

OLD RECTORY   So there can, there can.
[*He moves over to the table, and opens the box*]
I flick a switch, and this pyxiloquist,
This sound-book, legible to ears not eyes,
Plays back, *reviva voce*, all you've missed.
It is an artefact of rare device,
This product of the second Fall of Man,
So bear with me if I apostrophize
Its doomsday relic, and assess the price
It cost our kind. For its production meant
Not just that someone happened to invent
And someone make and someone market it.
Before these wheels could wind, this tape transmit
Its electronic parroting, the whole
Outlook of western man, his lofty bent
Of intellect and attitude of soul
In apposition to the infinite
Had to defect and suffer a descent
Down to the mundane, as he sought control
Not of himself but nature, and depressed
The journey that should be a pilgrim's quest
Into a power rush; narrowing his role
From Homo Sapiens to Man Techniscient.

RALPH
Wisdom or know-how – either in full growth
Excludes the other; since we can't have both,
He who computes, pollutes; in wisdom's lieu
Moon-trotter means globe-tribulator too.

DIRK

Science or soul? – a neo-Faustian pact
With Modimephistopheles, in fact.

RALPH

Who baited his new-fangled sorcery
(Based not on incantation but technique)
With such incentives, that our workshop-witted,
Contrivance-conscious forbears failed to see
Its implications till they were committed.
A proverb says the devil's boots don't creak.

OLD RECTORY

Well, we've agreed it was a costly toy,
Involving near-perdition – plague, that too.
Yet, since it's here, let's use it to enjoy
A repetition of the interview.
At least it can be said in such a ploy
We're giving Mephistopheles his due.
Shall I switch on?

DIRK   First, won't you introduce
The cast? To differentiate between
Three speeches, and decide whose voice is whose,
May not be simple when they can't be seen.

OLD RECTORY [*As he speaks he walks from one to
the other of the recumbent interviewers, indicating
each in turn*]
Yes, well suggested. Fossick, here, speaks first:
Their question-master, shrewd, professional;
Reality's his rock and fantasy
The sand we build in vain on – true for me
No less, our definitions being reversed.

Pinch-voiced, his tendency to cocknefy –
The kind of twang that once we used to call
Colonial (what darkness-years away!)
Is what at first you'll recognize him by.
Dic to his friends as Baytre here is Bay:
Their hermitage-collator, with a thirst
For rare examples – apt to get immersed
In rhapsodizings – voice pitched rather high,
Which makes him easy to identify.
So, by elimination, when you've heard
And marked the twang and treble, voice the third
You'll know is Ponder's – J.J. – here he is:
Their sub-interrogating *tertius quiz*;
A query-monger, one might say, who probes
Compulsively, his memory a kind
Of many-hangered wardrobe, which he hopes
To stock with new apparel for his mind.

DIRK

So that's the team. I find it hard to guess
Just how it came to be one, I confess.
I mean, how in that standstill world out there,
From one of its depopulated hives
Some stricken and depleted swarm could spare,
And not just spare – equip – three active lives
For so incongruous and prodigal
An expedition as a hermit-crawl.
This modern cult, this urge to interview,
How is it, that of all things, this survives
(And with its tape in working order, too)
From some technopolis the plague has sacked?

33

However much these urbanites once lacked
The wilderness, why need they now seek ours?
Their own surrounds them; desolate, intact
Street-miles without a face or wheel that drives;
Ghost-Broadways, where gaunt figures prowl or sit
Like Piranesi's, and below unlit,
Unheated but still lived-in dwelling-towers
Black rings of camp-fire scorch the pavement's flowers.
How can this dwindled remnant as it strives
To improvise, with sapped and meagre powers,
Some refugee existence, have the zest,
The curiosity, the interest,
The vigour to commission such a quest?

RALPH
Perhaps 'out there' has changed. Let's picture it
As two contrasted worlds. One, fallen apart
(As you've described): town deserts, droop and drift
Of sparse survivors, moribund, makeshift.
The other where, more resolute of heart,
A group, uniting, here and there contrives
To make in old surroundings a new start
Like settlers in a colony that thrives,
And shape existence back to its old form
(Except, as yet, there are no crowds to swarm).
And as this pre-plague way of life revives,
So, too, the impetus to look about
The post-plague world, explore it and find out
How neighbours fare; and thus a team is sent
Of interviewers to investigate
The flight to solitude and hermit-drain

Which in remoter wastelands, France and Spain,
As here, is rumoured to be prevalent;
And having picked on you through chance or fate,
It ends its mission at your garden gate.

OLD RECTORY

Chance? – why not Providence? In his designs
God (it's been said) draws straight with crooked lines.

*Here Old Rectory pauses, as if lost in speculation.
There is a silence, until eventually Dirk Willett recalls
the others to a previous point in the conversation.*

DIRK

Well, so much for digression. Back to you
And our dumb friends here waiting to discourse.
Your team-synopsis gave a vivid clue
To their three voices – quite a tour de force.
Let's hope the box won't make – it can't be new –
The fourth unrecognizable as yours.

OLD RECTORY

Let's hope its battery will stay the course
And not fade out before we're halfway through.

RALPH

Then turn the volume down and spare the horse.

OLD RECTORY

The volume? So.
[*He bends over the box and turns a dial*]
                    Shall I switch on?

RALPH   Ay.

DIRK   Do.

35

I watched them work it. Right – the INTERVIEW.

He presses a switch, watches, and quickly rejoins the other two, who have settled comfortably in their chairs. The three interviewers remain inert and immobilized.

SCENE III

FOSSICK

You're ready, rector? And the panel? So
I'll put the question which in every case
Has started our proceedings.

                         Rector, you,
As the last hermit to be interviewed,
What prompted you to seek the wilderness?
What over-riding urge was it that drew
Or drove you to select this lonely base
And live in self-inflicted solitude?

OLD RECTORY

A complex question – I should have to trace . . .

FOSSICK

Not too far back – no, don't mistake me, please –
It's merely that I'm anxious to avoid
One of those autoembryographies.

OLD RECTORY

I wasn't heading for the uterus.
Rousseau and Wordsworth are my Jung and Freud.
The origin I wanted to discuss
Was love of nature . . .

PONDER   May I intervene?
Such love of nature, as we've learnt, has been
A strong inducement – now and then, perhaps,
The main inducement – in the current phase
Of hermiting. But in the built-up scene
When you first sought, before the world's collapse,

Your haven, in those well-developed days
Exactly what did love of nature mean?

BAYTRE
It meant the love of countryside – excuse
My cutting in – by those who hungered still
To keep its precious scan, its cherished views
Unscathed, but lacked the vision and the will
To make the one essential sacrifice,
That is, to limit or forgo the use
Of gadgets that gave rise to ugliness,
Their workthings and their playthings – feebly loth
To drive one mile or turn one knob the less,
In hopes to have their cake and eat it too,
And serve god-Pan and Mammon-pylon both.
Result: the crumbled cake, the pyloned view.
Instead of countryside, an in-between
Of *rus in urbe* – greenbelt pastoral
With earshot traffic – and encroaching *urbs*
In rure – lanes with passing-bays and kerbs,
And scarlet kiosk on the village green,
And cottage shop's refrigerating hum,
And strip-lit smithy where the hunters come
On wheels – can you associate this all-
Modcons and love-of-nature compromise
With Wordsworth's creed and haunting waterfall?

OLD RECTORY
No more than, say, mastitis and the vet
With dairymaiding Marie Antoinette –
But . . .

38

BAYTRE
          Then your hermitage – was that some haunt
Deep valley-tucked, but handy for the jaunt
To town? Arcadian and undisturbed,
Yet up-to-date; beneath the blacksmith's latch
The locksmith's yale; the soil-pipe through the thatch,
And tell-tale grid upon the Tudor stack,
And tell-tale concrete drive-in to the back;
And where the view was, past a gnarled and fey
Peninsula of orchard trees that curbed
The frolic stream before it wound away,
Looped on black pole behind black pole behind
Black pole, the interloping wires that lined
Its long meanderings and didn't wind.

OLD RECTORY
You take one back to foregone days – to what
Might well have been some Georgian poet's cot,
Dorking or Ditchling – well, it wasn't mine.
My cottage shell, untenanted and tied
And due for demolition, stayed outside
– Though on the village outskirts – pipe and line.
I had its slates made waterproof, and then
Adding what was required to make it fit
For human occupancy, and remit
The demolition order, in my cell
I settled down, like Jung at Bollingen,
To seek the treasure spurned by modern men,
Simplicity; earth's water from a well,
Warmth from a wood, a garden and a goat
(Your words; it's by telepathy I quote).

39

BAYTRE

At least you were consistent – had the sense
To see that if you loathed the consequence
The obvious remedy was to abstain
From causing it, by use of switch and main
And gadgetry and teletry.

OLD RECTORY   A glutton
(You think) for abstinence, a Puritan
Troubled by scenic misdemeanours. No,
That mode of life was based on preference,
Not negative revulsion. I preferred
To any bulb or Belling instancy
My candles, kindly to the reading eyes,
That blended with instead of blotting out
The fireside's flicker to the further wall –
A simple blessing in a simple room,
Emblazoning its bareness. And I loved
To watch the four-cupped wrought-iron candlestick
Wax blond with tallow – kindling for the grate.
In the same way I would not have foregone
For all the taps in Chromia, the chore
That took me on dark mornings to the well,
This side or that of dawn, and as with crank
And creak of its old windlass I would haul
Up from a depth that made the very drips
Reverberate my climbing bucket clear,
Sometimes I'd glimpse, reflected in its load,
What seemed a silver minnow, the thin moon;
Or day's first cloud, a fluctuating rose.
Simple, inestimable. And I loved

The cheese I'd milked, the fire I'd sawn, the stew
I'd planted; loved the routine of a life
Shaped by such tasks, and worn into a gloss
By daily iteration – the same kind
Of homely patina that use had given
My shiny-handled spade. I loved as well
The indispensable, familiar few
Chattels I owned; on floor or shelf or hook
The landmarks of my indoor scenery,
Jug, skillet, basket, bowl, the haybox even . . .

    PONDER
Haybox? What's that?

    OLD RECTORY   An insulated bin
Or storage heater, where a boiling stew,
Once sealed, continued all night cooking in.

    PONDER
A simple gadget – did Jung have one, too?

    FOSSICK
We're drifting from the point. This country zest,
This love of nature which you then possessed
And which first prompted you to hermitize –
Tell us, how did it differ from that tame
Fervour – Bay's Pan-and-pylon compromise –
That love of nature later on became?

    OLD RECTORY
It was possession in a different sense –
I was possessed by it. For, suburb-bred,
I had a pavement boyhood. Larks for me
Were pranks, not birds. The apple-blossom's tinge
I never noticed; nor the change of sky

(The hoarding's change I did) except when clouds
Threatened a game of tennis, later golf.
(How far those pastimes make past times recede;
Remote as stoolball seems a stymie now).
My walks were shopwards, past the numbered gates
Of parlour-like front-gardens, privet-walled,
Down to the Broadway's fascia-fascination.
Summer meant longer days, and little else;
And when day switched to night, the evening star
Had no clear call for me; such things I missed,
And even puberty did not assist.
And when in manhood I became aware,
Belatedly and fervently aware
Of nature's loveliness, it was as if
I saw with the same eyes, but different sight,
Myself the convert, a converted world.
For if small things may be compared with great,
A country lane was my Damascus Road.

FOSSICK
And it was this experience, no doubt,
That prompted your self-exile.

OLD RECTORY   Exile? No,
Say rather my escape from exile, from
Confinement in the Siburberia
Of streets, its climate harsh with tarmac Junes
And privet Aprils. How it irked my spirit
To see a frost that whitened absent woods
Squander its scintillating treasury
On breakfast terraces; or misty shafts
Of soft October moonlight mock themselves

In lamp-post glades; or beautifying snow
Reverse its mask, and make a dreary street
More dreary, shovelled into grimey mumps.
I took to flight.

BAYTRE   And, as you have described,
Found your first cottage on a village fringe.

OLD RECTORY
And even there my cell would have become
As irksome as a prison's on fine days,
Had I been window-bound. No boon to me
To watch the autumn sunlight slowly shelve
Its vapour, if I watched it from a room.
I longed to be abroad and on the bank
Of gorse which spider-myriads had draped
In jewelled mist, unconsciously creating
Infinite riches with their little looms.
A rainbow always fetched me out of doors,
As if its spectrum were a spectacle
Too wide for windows, which I had to stand
And stare at in the open, and stare on
Until it dwindled to a coloured stub
Tingeing a tower. So, too, a likely cloud,
Serry or scud, would hurry me uphill
To watch its windy muster in the sky.
So, too, like times of festival for me
Were snow and mist and flood – for if I loved
The landscape as it was from day to day,
How much more, when they were enhancing it
With wooded whiteness or swathed distances
Or fields that ferried a reflected swan.

43

All day was then a walk: trudge, pause and stare,
An eager strider up each hill, and on
Its brow an eager statue; and, perhaps,
When home I'd plodded, just at candle time
And taken to my fireside, the glimpsed moon
Rising, would fetch me out to gaze again,
Entranced and rivetted, until my viewing
Became a kind of vigil, and I longed
For some quick cloud to edge across the night
And moon go in, so I could go in too.

BAYTRE
Yes, there's a burden even in delight,
That artists feel, a sense of travail . . .

OLD RECTORY   Say
Of contest, even; for it sometimes seemed
As if I wrestled with the Beauty there,
Like Jacob with the angel.

PONDER   Jacob who?

BAYTRE
Of contest? – call it that if harvest's one.
Not pitching sheaves but garnering impressions
With no less toil. But did you never work
Directly, canvas propped against the view?

OLD RECTORY
My mode was more Chinese: the artist-sage
Who sat for six months cross-legged in Szechwan,
Nor put a brush to silk; but carried home
Creative ponderings that had absorbed
The Eternal Tao into locality,

44

And there depicted them with hand and soul.
I only claim the mode, not the achievement.

FOSSICK

Well, you achieved at least a livelihood.

OLD RECTORY

A livelihood! What, I – with my returns
To Turner, and my on-beat Constables!
I! in those aababstractcoram days,
Art without form and Freud. I only had
Two customers: the bonfire and the stack.

FOSSICK

How then – and here I hope you will forgive
A private question – I would not intrude it
But it's a stock one – how then did you live?

OLD RECTORY

The answer's private, too: on private means.

PONDER

An income from the source you so deplored:
Megapolis; shops, factories, machines?

OLD RECTORY

No, not exactly income; say a hoard.
I realized my assets – it seemed best –
Like Pope the poet's father, who, precluded
As Papist from all right to re-invest
His business proceeds, locked them in a chest
And lived on them, retired. I've done the same.

BAYTRE

And did you bring it with you, when you came –
Your wooden wallet – to the wilderness?

45

OLD RECTORY
My wooden wallet, as you term it – yes.
Where it has nourished, like the widow's cruse,
Myself and my three colleagues.

PONDER   But – excuse
My cutting in – a way of life like yours,
Doesn't this taint it at the very source,
Brand it with inconsistency?

OLD RECTORY   Of course –
Or would do if we ever claimed we sought
A way of life, not just a way of thought.

PONDER
Even so, for hermits . . .

FOSSICK   I don't wish to block
Discussion, but we must observe the clock.
By now we should have reached the hermitage –
Instead . . . So tell us of the second stage
Of your removal, rector. Was it God
Or Nature gave the call, or man the prod
That drove you from your village life, or drew?

PONDER
To-ite or from-ite, rector: which were you?

OLD RECTORY
Seeker or fugitive? As you suggest,
To shun and seek are both the hermit's lot.
And my first choice of cottage, neighbour-fringed,
Turned out to be a bad one. I had got
If not the worst, at least the second-best
Of both worlds. For the village-world impinged

(A life like mine was easy to distract),
Yet compensating company it lacked.
A solitary without a solitude,
I'd found seclusion that did not seclude.

PONDER
Impinged – in what way?

OLD RECTORY   Dogs.

PONDER   Dogs?

OLD RECTORY   Dogs. You know
How the Plague brought–since they were not attacked–
A plague of dogs, marauding strays, that packed
In gangs of four or five – you must have seen
Such on your way here, foraging for food
Round copse or clamp, Alsatian, Aberdeen,
And every colour, shape and breed between.
Well, long before the Plague, my cottage gate
Attracted such a mob, at woof and wait
And woof for every tradesman's come and go:
A pest of loose-end pets, a roadside bane
Of yappersnappers – how, they barked at me,
Tray, Blanch and Sweet-heart.

BAYTRE   Could you not complain?

OLD RECTORY
Complain! I lived in a canocracy
Which had abolished kennel, whip and chain.
Dog was its palindrome.

PONDER   To balance that
Were there no neighbours whom you cared to see
And talk with; get to know and so get known?

47

OLD RECTORY

My hermit-views were very much my own;
And if I shared them, was there any ground
For hope I'd find agreement or agree?
Besides, I felt – no doubt mistakenly –
The human scenery was tame and flat
And featureless; no lofty rise and fall
Of aspiration, but a dull terrain
Of trivial concerns and topical
Pre-occupations. What could I have found
Conversable in neighbours topic-bound
By gadgetry and teletry?

FOSSICK   Concede
That you were not gregariously inclined.

OLD RECTORY

Gregariously! Do you expect to find
Say, Jeremiah clubbable; or, say,
Cassandra a soroptimist?

FOSSICK   Agreed –
But they were not misanthropists.

OLD RECTORY   Was I?
Ask Dirk, ask Ralph, ask even Malachi;
My friends, whose lives are facing the same way.
My neighbours faced the other, unaware
Of drift or danger. Nothing isolates
Like a foreboding, which no others share
Of doom, where everyone participates
In the doomed system. I alone could hear,
It seemed, the future roaring in the weir.

The stream itself was swift enough and strong
Without the adverse jostle of a throng
Of drifters down. I found, as in my art,
Who swims against the stream must swim apart.

PONDER
You'd say the dog-mob plus the dearth of men
Were the main from-ite factors?

OLD RECTORY   Plus the Wen.

PONDER
The what?

OLD RECTORY The meganormity that came
Close to my favourite valley's end, and took
Its terminating fringes for a frame.
The tiny Eden of a single brook
It seemed, that valley, and the brook revealed
Its whole course in one view – from where the brown
Of hillside bracken hinted at its source,
To where it reached and re-appeared beyond
A furlong coombe, to where a watermill's
Sluices and dykes still passed it through a pond,
(The millhouse lived in but no longer wheeled)
To where it picked a lane up in its course
That wound beside it only slightly less
Through those sequestered grazings: cloth of gorse
Draping a golden acre like a gown
On one steep slope; but mostly pasture hills
With skyline sheep and clambers of dark hedge
And coppice up their green declivities.
It was on one of such – an emerald edge
That jutted out like a diminutive down –

49

I had my belvedere, and could survey
Upstream and down, the valley either way,
And at its lower end, the open plain.
Here, as one day I watched,
(After some absence – illness like as not)
I watched in horror and amazement. What
Could be going on there? Vehicle and crane,
Scaffold and scoop. A thousand acre plot
Void of one vestige of a tree, and blotched
With dump and hutment. How take in the size
And scope of that Pharaohic enterprise,
Which grew and grew, until it seemed as if
The very skyline by the imposition
Of stack colossus and asbestos cliff
Had been eroded? When at length a whiff
Fumed from its crater, it was the emission
Of no volcano's cauldron, but a white
Bulge-blight of nightmare height, a moloch shape
That could have turned into a horrorscape
The flattest vista, scaringly out of scale
On steppe or prairie, for my hill and dale,
So gently, congruously curved, a crude
Obliteration. How could I have viewed
Its presence there undaunted; or subdued
Its anti-vision by my strength of vision?
I called to mind how, peering at the rain
I sheltered from, once in some tottered shed,
Through the bleared window with its spidery skein
I saw a rainbow; as I ducked my head
To leave, saw too, emerging from the floss,
A black bunch leg it loathsomely across

The bright bridge: Satan in Eve's Paradise,
Moloch in mine – there were affinities.
At least it drove me out; a kind of dread
Mingled with my abhorrence, and I fled.

FOSSICK
Fled – shall we say, escaped? Don't you agree
What you withdrew from was reality?
Nature, encroached on in so many ways,
Was doomed (or so, in that progressive phase
Before the Plague, it seemed). By your retreat
You sought, before encroachment was complete,
Some haven, where you could live out your dream.
And yet you claimed to swim against the stream.

OLD RECTORY
Reculer pour mieux nager. Still, I own
I laid my treasure up in scenery;
That is, on earth, where blight (not moth) and din
(Not rust) corrupted; and land-thieves broke in
And stole (their plans approved). Had Wordsworth
        known
The Lakes in tourist times, would even he
Have worshipped still the splendour in the grass
Round Caffmere, Speedwater and Picnic Pass?
Our shrines were vulnerable; and not just
To those equivalents of moth and rust
Which were but symptoms, symptoms of malign
Autonomy within, the outward sign
Of human life discarding the divine.
That was the crux; how in a world astray
(I with it) find the way back to the Way,

The Truth, the Life? It was astray indeed:
Foundered on fact; the way of vision blocked
By Freudian veto; every value rocked
By anti-value; crisis in the creed
Where even belief in God was found to be
– By priests – an obsolete fidelity;
In Jesus – by his own Society.
What else, in such a flux, remained to do
But substitute the desert for the church,
And undertake, apart, a one-man search
For the false turning, and so find the true?
To-ite, you ask, or from-ite? I withdrew
To hermit-life, impelled by this deep need.
Then came the Plague, and hermit-life indeed.

FOSSICK

That answers our main question. Quite a stage
It's been, this journey to your hermitage.
Now we've arrived, the others should not take
So long to cope with. I propose a break.

SCENE IV

The same. The recording comes to a stop: and as Old
Rectory goes over, he pauses to look at the three
recumbent investigators.

OLD RECTORY
They liked the drink I gave them – said they knew
That monks had brandied herbs to make Chartreuse
And Benedictine – but that hermits too
Concocted their own aromatic brew
They'd never guessed – called it Old Hermitage,
And sipped down hibernation with its grape:
My time-drug, with an action I could gauge
To work just when I wanted. Not one stirs:
Had Circe dormice, these could have been hers;
Exempt till morning! Let me change the tape.

He returns to his seat, having done this; and the
recorded interview continues.

SCENE V

FOSSICK

Having moved on to ask what moved you on,
Our second question follows from the first:
Your credo. In a world that's come of age
Like ours, how was it, rector, you reversed
Your love of nature, which we still can share,
To love of God, a long outmoded stage?
Your fields that ferried a reflected swan
Are our Elysian Fields. If faith once blew
Bright bubbles, floating in life's after-air,
Science has pricked them; and you can't unburst
More than a bubble a pricked point of view;
Or modernize the medieval stare
For which the seraph in the dreamsud flew.
For us the galaxies alone are there.
Heaven? The lens at Jodrell wonders where.

OLD RECTORY

Surely reflectors don't reflect like that,
Though once I did myself, when all my care
Was care for nature; since, although this had
Akin to piety a zeal intense
That had come on me like a second birth
Leading to worship, yet my only sense
Of the unearthly was in terms of earth
(Reducing Heaven to a landscape phrase).
As when, against a sombre sky-back, rays
Of evening glory, dazzling through a rift,
Make the woods virid with a green not May's:

Unearthly groves. Or when the moonlit shift
Of storms disclosed the night sky silver-cliffed:
Unearthly alps. Enrapt by all I saw,
So vividly, spectacularly there,
Small wonder that I stood and stood, not awe-
But beauty-struck, on Plato's bottom stair.

PONDER
And when you climbed, what was it drove or drew?

OLD RECTORY
My credo had defects.

PONDER   And those were?

OLD RECTORY   Two:
Vulnerability, inadequacy.
And vulnerable upon a double ground:
Submersion from without, by jet or wen,
Grid, tarmac, chainsaw – and even if I found
Intact seclusion, might that bring no less
Atrophy from within; and my response
Of rapture to the landscape's loveliness
Deaden, as Ruskin's did to Coniston's?
Suppose, alert as ever, it lived on –
My foreground had no figures, and would rocks
Show me solicitude, the whispering breeze
Listen as I did, or the moonlit storm
Invigorate my shoulders for the shocks
That even solitary flesh is heir to,
Or help me curb its lusts, St Anthony's?
And if inadequate for life, still more
For death: then, then, what re-assurance then

Could Nature give, to brace me to prepare to
Become a husk and perish? She'd perform
Her task, collect the refuse from the bone,
Indifferent quite, whether the lonely one
Who was her priest continued to adore,
Or merely witness as a skeleton.

PONDER
So, shunning men, you found your nature-creed
Deficient too.

OLD RECTORY I came to feel the need
For consolation and to feel the lack
Of a Consoler. Cogitating back
On why and when the cleavage came, the rift
With God – how would this look in retrospect
I wondered? Would it really prove to be
That Man the child, through all his history
The child, had in a century or two
(Wen-centuries, all faith and morals wrecked)
Grown into Man the man? Or what he knew
As Truth, Truth making all religious doubt
Undoubted, would not this appear in turn
truth that came in with Newton and went out
With Einstein, coinciding with a shift
In human consciousness, as man's concern
Became absorbed by gene and galaxy
So totally, they seemed totality?
What if all-History had indeed been right,
And Man the child a sage, and Man the man
A know-more who'd manipulated lessness?
What if, engrossed by power, he'd made a pact

Like Faust, and disinherited his soul
From Heaven, to lodge bodies on the moon?
What if 'what if' were the equivalent
In times of doubting to *le grand peut-être*
In times of faith . . . ? And in such case, what if
Behind all worlds there were indeed a Will,
And order supernatural to ours
In which the morning stars once sang together
And all the sons of God shouted for joy?
And when my valley's shadow turned to dark
What if I should find solace in a psalm?

PONDER
And so you saw the light. Was this a flash
Of vision or a kind of gradual dawn?

OLD RECTORY
Not even dawn – more like an intimation.
To hear me prate you'd think the Heavens opened
As once to Handel, when he filled them with
The Hallelujah Chorus. But before
Reality began to re-exist,
And I to realize that I had missed
All through my life life's only mattering fact,
Time passed. I groped my way up Plato's stair . . .
Until at last . . . But how describe the Word
In words? Sufficient that the wilderness
Remained no more the visible all-in-all
That with myself made up the scheme of things.
Though still the foreground to my solitude,
The inexpressible adjacency
Of Heaven made it also foreground to

The Kingdom and the Glory and the Power
Not of this universe, exalting it
So that it blossomed like a rose derived.
And how much more a sterile desert seemed
The Cities of the Wen that I, like Lot,
Had fled from; in what contrast to my peace
Their strident-streeted techni-termitaries,
A nemesystem with the doom built in,
Speedebriation, mammonotony,
Crisis and craving its doomsdaily life.

PONDER

Doomed? And if doomed, had not God's hand in that
A finger too? Grant a Creator – where
The Shepherd, Father of your psalm and prayer?
My version of apocalypse might be
A vision of divine satiety.
I'd see our world, still populous, go phut,
Go up in smoke, as if with all its rough,
Sad, splendid history in the heavens set,
It was a kind of cosmic cigarette
Which He who rolled it had enjoyed enough.
He takes a final puff
And into chaos throws away the butt.

FOSSICK

J.J. on Patmos! If I may recall
My earlier question – in supernal air
We've wandered somewhat – and resume from there.
You grant, if Christians are imparadised
With resurrected-in-the-body Christ,
Their heaven must have dimension.

58

OLD RECTORY   I agree.

FOSSICK
Then give it a location. By the Bear?
In inexpressible adjacency
To the third twinkle on Orion's belt?
Prior to science, when believers knelt,
Without abuse of sense they could assume
That somewhere beyond elsewhere there was room
For a celestial somewhere else. Can we?
Hope like St Paul for Heaven against hope,
We surely can't against the telescope.

OLD RECTORY
Your science – is it Einstein post- or pre-?
If post, what problem? Pre, men came to view
Nature as a materiality
Of Heaven-excluding star-stuff spreading through
Limitless space. No room for angels there:
Lens-eyed astronomers eliminate
Their legions at a look. Then Einstein came
And saw and pondered: and our universe
(Or model of it that approximates)
Reveals a system energies create
By interacting to compose a frame
Or web. And space-time's all-exclusiveness
Is gone. Since other systems, better, worse,
Could coexist with ours; and even be
As physical as ours; while utterly
Distinct from ours – mysterious alternates
To make a multiverse (again our guess

59

At how the frame of matter is designed
Owing its emergence to a frame of mind).

FOSSICK

So Einstein by-passes astronomy?
Grant it, if only for that hoary sake
The argument's – and where's your evidence
As to what form such otherness would take?
Einstein or not, your Heaven still can be
A compensation-dream, a psychic fake
Of fantasy that fear of death invents.

OLD RECTORY

And why do men fear death? But let's move on,
And take the products. For it's surely odd
That when in backward times deluded men
Imagined a vain thing, and worshipped God
Or gods, they built a Wells or Parthenon
Or other lovely fanes of falsehood. Then,
As creeds dispersed and Truth unclouded shone,
The temple was . . . well, I've described the Wen.

FOSSICK

That merely shows the incidence of art.
Does Athens prove Athene, Chartres make sense
Of the Annunciation? Evidence
Like that will hardly give your case a start.

OLD RECTORY

Then take the mystics, men of varied creed
And country, sprinkled over every age,
Saint, sufi, rabbi, guru, poet, sage,
Plotinus, Laotze, Dante, Eckhart, Paul,

Isaiah, Al-Ghazzali, men who all
(Vedanta and Apocalypse) agreed
In their experience of some sublime
Participation that transcended time
And creed and country. From so wide a range
Of human contrast, does it not seem strange
The testimonies were identical
Of what they reached and where?

FOSSICK   Strange? Why? Did all
Not have a common origin, the same
Sump of the soul, from which subconscious void
Illusions of beatitude emerge
As sublimations of the sexual urge?
If Heaven exists, from that subliminal
Kingdom it comes. I trump – to win the game –
Your Einstein ace, and take the trick with Freud.

OLD RECTORY
No, have-it-both-ways sir, in playing the hand
– Look – you revoked. No room, you say, up there
For Heaven: all telescopically scanned
Light-years of star-stuff. Then, without a blush
Or blench, into my body-stuff, my strut
Of bones, dissectable anatomy
Of organs, heart-pump, bladder's cistern-flush,
Lung-bellows and computer-occiput
You tacitly intrude a – kingdom. Where?

FOSSICK
A kingdom?

OLD RECTORY
                    That was your word – mine would be
A continent, a New World, with its own
Dream-scenery and under-eyelid sky:
Own language, hieroglyphics of the couch;
Own elemental forces, storing up
Mysterious promptings; own mythology,
Libido, Censor, Superego, Id
And Oedipus; its guardian Archetypes,
And Zeitgeist, bearing messages from all
Men living, as Ancestral Memory
Men dead – this psyche, this pre-ceptacle
Of guilts, gods, Muses, *angst* and *déjà vu*,
Prayers, premonitions, this cosmopolis
In which all people that on earth do dwell,
Or ever did, seem somehow to be present
You lodge in my physique. Inform me where.
Fix a location for it. By my ear?
In inexpressible adjacency
To the third button of my trouser belt?
Instruct me.

   FOSSICK   Are you meaning to imply
That soul in man and Heaven in the sky
Are in some sort analogous?

   OLD RECTORY   Don't press
The parallel. I'm merely trying to stress
That both within us and without are queer
Cosms of mystery, beyond the peer
Of bronchi- as of telescope; and – yes,
I'll say it – that you seem to understand

Their secret much as flies do when they land
Upon – let's say a score of Bach, and treat
The fugue there as the ground beneath their feet.

BAYTRE

The fugue? One hermit whom we interviewed
Possessed a clavichord, which he had made
Himself. Its tinklings in that solitude
Were like a redbreast's plaintive serenade
That seems to autumn August.

PONDER   In this mood
You came to be a Christian?

OLD RECTORY   Mood? Not quite.
But may we, if we meet to-morrow night,
Discuss that later? For today let's pause
At my first groping after the First Cause,
Which led me to acknowledge (groping still)
That if what once was called primeval slime
(In current jargon, pre-biotic soup)
Evolved in course of aeons to a group
Playing Beethoven, it needed more than time
And chance, it needed a creative will
To foster that emergence, and express
Amoeba as A Minor. So for me
Religion entered nature. Stream and tree
Retained their old enchantment, cloud and hill
Their beauty, but with that of holiness
Evident too; as when the sunset told
The time on the church clock in hands of gold.

SCENE VI

FOSSICK

Well, thank you, rector: leave off where you like.
A pity we should have to do so just
As your church clock appeared about to strike –
Still, if we must, we must.
And since our own clock has some time to spare,
Would you, before we end our interview
(Before, I mean, this session of it ends),
Deal with two questions which I know our friends
Here long to ask.

OLD RECTORY What are they?

FOSSICK   A stock pair:
The Simple Life dilemma; and what we
Have classified as the St Anthony
Syndrome.

OLD RECTORY And called the devil's tempt-in.

FOSSICK   Eh?

OLD RECTORY
Venice and Venus . . . ? Hm. Well, ask away.

BAYTRE
Who mentioned Venice?

OLD RECTORY   You did; but don't press,
Don't press me how. Let's say, a lucky guess.

Or an inspired one. Rector, when you drew
Your cottage-portrait, with its well's-eye view
Of 'day's first cloud, a fluctuating rose',
It struck a chord, but struck a discord, too.
The Simple Life – fine, fine; but if pursued
As an ideal, and not just by you
But men in general, must it not deplete,
Discourage, even in the end preclude
What I most prize, creative plenitude?
St Peter or St Peter's? Follow him
And Rome reverts to village. Music goes,
Art, drama, architecture. Mozart's bow
Fiddles a folk-tune only. Vanbrugh plans
In thatch. Cellini models pots and pans.
Exeunt Shakespeare and Euripides.
Or take the two reflections: yours we know,
The bucket's; mine your lucky guess foresees,
That city's with a stretch of mirrored sky
Azure-apparent in its every street,
Where cloud above and marble at the brim
Mingle reflections, and the sunset's rose
May, in the shimmer, or may not be glows
From a pink palace. Verity or vision?
In Turner-light a vision from the sea
Embellishing the sunrise, lapis-lapped
And dewy-domed, its fabulous façade
In golden haze, a mirage-miracle –
Yet still a city – seen with what precision
In Canaletto's focus, as he drew
Those still-same scenes ourselves once floated through

Eye-avid, and revealed that verity
Itself in Venice was a kind of vision,
Requiring only a consummate lens
To show it; show a single work of art
Could be a city; show the sparkling sense
Of light and magical amenity
That went with streets of down-to-water walls
Made timeless by the tide; show, at its heart,
The basin of St Mark's, the travellers' dream,
Bucentaur and the wedding to the sea,
And pride of famous landmarks, shapes supreme
Almost congesting with magnificence
Lagoon and skyline, that made Venice seem
The world's *mirabile visu* – even the throng
Of traffic and dark ply of vehicles
A lesser glory, gondoliered along.
So much for my reflections. These, all these,
Your simple life, content with simple beauty,
Would willingly forgo, allow to fail:
Dome, doge, and campanile and Salute,
The cloud-lapped towers, the gorgeous palaces
Diminished to a dawn flush in a pail.

OLD RECTORY

The Campanile – how I loved that view
Of its grand shaft across the paved perfection
Fourth-sided by St Mark's – the maestro's too,
Or was it Guardi's? A strange recollection
For me, here; even perhaps, post-plague, for you.
Venice was your dilemma's gilded horn.
Its bare one . . . ? In Assisi I found both:
The shed where poverty was preached in love;

And, monasteried on the hill above,
Wide walls with Giotto's frescoes round – a growth
Of no-expense-spared architecture, born
In paradox. How was I to assess
Them, reconcile the monumental scheme
Of art, the hovel site of holiness?
Yet, if the saintly vision was supreme,
Did it make creativity grow less?
Had Giotto not made poverty his theme,
Art would have been the poorer. And the Rood,
The Crib – have these depleted plenitude?
And how much of the greatest art derives
A lustre from the humblest of all lives,
Christ, Buddha, saints?

    PONDER [*half-aside*] Even one day, at a guess,
St Rectory.

    OLD RECTORY Pah!

    BAYTRE   It's not that you assign
Supremacy, it's your exclusive line,
Rector, that I'm concerned with. Show me why
Your life, the simple one, must so extend
Its claim, and thread us through its needle's eye,
It seems to sidetrack the creative, mine.
Aren't both vocations valid? Why confine
To one the wings of worship, and imply
The other misses life's authentic end?

    OLD RECTORY
No way of life's authentic as an end.
Make creativity the final end
Of god-forsaking Man, and in the end

It is not Venice that you'll get, my friend,
But the power-polyp at my valley's end,
And technomania about to end
A plenty-stricken world. End is divine.
Life not all heyday; it involves as well
A bridge of sighs to death – perhaps to Hell.
And even Venice, in its haze of gold,
Not always made the heart feel, we've been told,
Jubilant. Sometimes, chilly and grown old.
So did not feel St Francis.

                       Now your next
And final question. Why of death (to quote
A less despondent text) begin a tale?
We're faced with life and Ponder: life that's sexed
And vulnerable; Ponder who's perplexed
And venerable – not I mean in years
But pedigree, all asking and all ears
Like old Herodotus, upon the trail
Of truth, a gowned interrogation note.
So now he comes to probe us, and compare
Then with now hermits, all agog to gauge
How far temptation in the hermitage
Is still endemic. Back in far-gone days,
If in the desert some abandoned fort
Or palace stood, where (in Isaian phrase)
The satyr, among stones of emptiness,
Cried to his fellow, such was deemed the lair
Of demons and their privileged resort.
Hence in the Bosch Temptation the saint prays
Not by his cave, but in a castle court:
Hallucination architectural

Of runic ruin; weird arcaded wall
(With fiends that flicker in its haunted bays)
Above an opposite-to-Lethe lake
Where swimmers, with bewildered bob-heads, wake
Not from but into dreams, a miscreation
Of freak forms, nightmare unworld of mutation.
Above, the anchorite averts his eyes
(Though not his fantasies) and seeks relief
From diabolic hybrids that entice
And pester him with the make-misbelief
Of a Black Mass they gibber mummering.
Elsewhere the artist – in the triptych wing –
Depicts him as if struggling to withstand
Thoughts that would pry behind the figleaf hand
Of a nude temptress. Bodily frustration
Ferments in soul, libido with its wand
Concocting sinscape; and, in woods beyond,
His hermitage, half torso and half tor,
Crouches alive, with shoulder fields that rise
To hillock buttocks, the supporting thighs
Strangely portcullarsed, to denote a door.
Such the 'then' picture. Does the 'now' that's ours
Differ so far, as, like St Anthony,
We grapple with the seven deadly powers –
And deadliest for us the hermit's three,
Greed, lust and sloth . . . ?

    PONDER   Not differ? In one thing
Clearly it differs. Whereas Bosch brings in
A supernatural agent to incite
And tempt, for us temptation seems to be
Mainly a reflex of the appetite;

Since rebel flesh will always have its fling,
Or try to, if repressed by penancing.
If this distracts the soul, fermenting it,
Must we imagine, when you're lured by sin
To tipple berry-sherry, or admit
Fantasturbatory soliciting
Of sex, that in a guilty trance you're hauled
Aloft, *peccavi*-conscious and appalled
By demons?

OLD RECTORY That's not Bosch, it's Grunewald.

PONDER
At any rate, it's demons.

OLD RECTORY   And for you
Demons are Bosch. Well, even if that's true,
Was he so wide, I wonder, of the mark?
For if his demonstrosities aren't real,
They are surreal, the equivalent
Of forces from the subworld of the self,
Dream-peepholed and dream-peopled; taking shape
As complexes and traumas, phobias,
Delusions, guilts, libidinosities,
Distractions popping up to pimp our prayers;
Fixations in the psyche that obsess
The inner scen'ry, desolating it
With perpendicular appalling cliffs
Of scree-desertion, or transforming to
Obscenery, gloat, priapicturesque,
Rumps, humps and stumps. If, then, the soul's assailed
Not from without by demons, but (as monstrous)
By Freudian irrationalities

That vex it from within; and if of these
Sex is the source and *primum mobile ;*
And if the hermit, more than other men,
Is conscious of them through that inward eye
That can be the curse, too, of solitude –
Was the 'then' picture of the Antonine
Temptation so unlike the 'now' that's mine?
And Bosch's demonology, his dark
Soulscape so wide, I wonder, of the mark?

PONDER
You drag in the subconscious, rector – why?
For if such hermits all were on the run
From sex, and carried with them memories
Of what they fled from, would it not be these
– Their recollections of things seen or done
Once in the sex-pit – they'd be tempted by –
Or haunted, rather? Pages that pursue
From books read furtively, or frontal hair
Once peeped at in a pornshop; even pew
Equivocal, or pulpit, even prayer
To those of them recalling, as I do,
That press report of a redundant church
Converted to a discotheque, but still
Keeping its character, to add the thrill
Of sacrilege; with go-go altar girls,
Provocatively surpliced; phallic font:
Lessons from Lawrence, with the bishop's blessing
Read for a laugh; indecorous décor:
Frescoes of topless angels, Onan, Lot,
And Satan's exploits as an incubus.

Surely, if they were subject to assault
By such lewd promptings through the memory . . .

Here the voice fades out. Old Rectory goes to the apparatus, fiddles with it, taps it, shakes it, and then turns to his fellow hermits.

SCENE VII

OLD RECTORY
Assault! He should have added battery.
Dead – not a spark. So there it is, my friends;
As far as you're concerned, the session ends.

RALPH
Have we missed much?

OLD RECTORY   A Fossick thrust about
The hermit-life being one of fantasy,
And how my Bosch admission bore this out.
I parried; we agreed to disagree;
At least, until I offered a last drink,
Which was effective.
                              So, what did you think
Of the performance?

DIRK   Briefly, much too long.
And lengthy as it was, with all that to-
And-fro of question-answer, ding and dong,
I can't see that it got you anywhere.

OLD RECTORY
Why, after all, it was an interview;
They chose the questions.

DIRK   And up Plato's stair
You groped the answers. I'll at least concede
You didn't build cathedrals in the air.
Your Apologia of life and creed,
Viewed as an edifice, appeared to end
With the foundations.

73

OLD RECTORY   That's the crux, God knows.
For in the modern mindquake, even those
Have been erupted. It's our Christian plight;
Before re-building we must clear the site.

RALPH
In my view, Luke – or must you be addressed
As rector? – in my view you cleared it well:
Perhaps too well. It struck me as I heard –
Or overheard – your argument unwind,
That sometimes you were too much at your best
Where it least mattered; and the dazzle blurred
What mattered most. It put me in the mind,
Or fancy rather, of some Book of Hours
In which the borders of grotesques and flowers,
Monkey and mermaid, caterpillar, gem
And peacock have such gusto, they dispel
All thoughts of Calvary and Bethlehem –
So you, with dogs, with Venice. Best can be,
In the wrong place, a blemish.

OLD RECTORY   I agree.
But then my whole performance was a flaw
In some respect. For though it helped prepare
Subliminal misgivings, not a straw
Did any of them on the surface care
For my grand prate (Aquinas' straw to me?).
And had they seemed convinced (as they did not)
I still should wonder – of precisely what
I had convinced them. God's Reality?
Or that an old recluse they'd come to see,
A phoneyfogey, was convinced of such?

74

So much for dialectic; and so much
For session one. I'd hoped to-morrow night's,
Up at the church there, would set all to rights.
Then no more talk or gagarrulity,
I thought; for with your help and Malachi's
I'd cast to conjure up, by tapping springs
Of psi-suggestion – with a herb or so
My charismatic wand of Prospero –
A kind of masque or vision, and devise . . .
But pointless now for you to get to grips
With mode and means. At least I hoped you'd see
My edifice, as you have termed it, rise
Above foundation level and reveal –
Through a fresh medium – the verities
Of death, redemption and Apocalypse,
As in our creed; to such effect that these
Inquisitive, inquisitorial three
Who came to interview remained to kneel:
Reversion, not conversion. Deity
Abides; a psychic shift, and men conclude
That God has changed, not just their attitude
To God. In these I planned to change it back,
And set them on the archetypal track
We have retrieved out here. Inoculate
With truth, the desert serum.
Such was my scheme, when in a band of three
I saw them . . . and foresaw them from my gate
Depart, involuntary colporteurs . . .

RALPH
Such was? You're not proceeding with it?

75

I shall abandon it and let them go.
I hoped to use their visit; now I see
Providence meant their visit to use me,
And send, instead of them, the three of us.
It's often been our custom to discuss
The likelihood that one day, all or each
Would go back to the world, to found or preach:
Preach the old faith, found new communities.
The desert lacked a summons. Here it is.
This foolish interview has had the power
To jolt our day-to-dayness, and so primed
Us into act. They wished (said one) my tower
With sunset on its golden hands had chimed –
So, in a sense, it has. Let's not defer.
And as before, when human history
Seemed at its nadir, the inert, corrupt,
Gross and yet grandiose, world-lumbering lump
Of Rome was vivified by that small speck
Of gospel leaven, and through age-long working
Of faith in ferment, suffered a see-change,
Circus to Sistine, may not we, a tiny
Speck of that speck, now yeast the nadir lump
In slump out there, and so prepare a base
For a new world, a world of simpler shape
And outlook, grounded in redemptive grace;
From which a thousand wonders, like this tape,
Have lapsed, unwanted, even perhaps abhorred;
But with the sense of wonder in their place
Revived, the Way pursued, the Life adored,
And to the soul its destiny restored?

EPILOGUE
in Seven Scenes

SCENE I

*Having decided to abandon the wilderness and return
to the world, Old Rectory and his fellow hermits leave
the interviewers still sleeping in the house, and walk up
through the moonlit garden to the church, where they
are to make a farewell visit. As they climb to the terrace,
Old Rectory explains his reason for proposing this.*

OLD RECTORY
Name, fame, posterity – such brags have passed,
(The breakfast fan-fare) – we gaze up, not on;
No progress but the pilgrim's. And although
I made the church up here my studio,
My studio has still remained a church,
Easel and altar never far apart.

RALPH BROMPTON RALPH
A sanctum in both senses – even from us
Kept private.

OLD RECTORY
Though we met on the same search
Our modes were different – yours to pray and fast,
While I, co-seeker in a world unmapped
Almost as chaos, neither sage nor saint,
I found, as well you know and understand,
My *via speculandi* in my art,
Pictor devotus, pondering in paint
On the soul's errand, work half pigment and
Half mahlstick meditation. Poring thus
With palette, as I tussled to adapt

A Paradise by Fra Angelico,
My brushwork brushed beatitude; or hand,
Depicting Calvary, instructed heart
That my Redeemer liveth.
                              So, friends, so
If now, on this last night before we go
Back to the flux, I take you on a tour
Of my pew gallery, a last look round
(For you a first), it's not to yearn and grieve
For cherished ploys, or sheet up and secure
From the owl's droppings, then take saddened leave.
If one or two we canvass, one or two
Of my key canvases, it is to stamp
The stages (each a picture) on my mind
Of that long pilgrimage, the onward tramp
Back to reality – thus, having found
Journey's end here, these markers (left behind)
I'll carry in my consciousness, when you
And I out there re-visit, in its need,
A world collapsed and lapsed, post-plague, post-creed.

RALPH
Men only understand what they create
(It's said). Since your concerns were human fate,
The facts of death, redemption, Judgement, so,
Puzzling these out in paint, you came to know
Their nature.

DIRK WILLETT
                    Nature, or their nature – which?
If, on your advent here, you were possessed
By Nature, when the hermit in you soared
From that to heaven, could the artist switch

His range so readily ? With what a zest
Of skill and faculty you may have viewed
The terrace here and stretch of solitude,
Your talent's territory – with what loss
Of aptitude the Cross.

OLD RECTORY
Well, since it was the hermit who explored,
The artist acting only as a bridge,
Expect no masterpieces – merely free
Sub-renderings of such. Come on, you'll see
Soon what I mean.

DIRK   And yet before we do,
Let's take a last – it well may be our last –
Look at this other kind of picture, where
The moon, with its investiture of night,
Glorifies every cloud and all we view.
Calm, lovely, magical, immaculate –
How well that stray line from some buried bard
Sums up the silver changeling and its spell
So absolute, yet so susceptible
To alien intrusion.

RALPH   As out there
We'll soon perhaps encounter, glare and blare
Of a reverting stridency, marred, jarred
By sodium and neon, jazz and juke.
Or, if our commune picks a country site,
A lamp post on the lawn, lit up before
Moonrise, or naked bulb by the front door.

OLD RECTORY
Even here some such suburban relic stood.

I creepered it, in hope to make its hood
A nesting-box.

    RALPH   Your only nestlings, Luke,
Are where we left them, safely drugged below
Your rectory rooftop.

    DIRK   Rooftop – as we passed
The yew hedge, did you notice how it cast
Sharp chimney-shadows there? Or, further on,
With what a ghostly tinge the brickwork shone
Almost subdued to silver, as it spread
With just a glimmer of nocturnal red
Round the walled garden?

    RALPH   Did you ever try
For such effects on canvas – Turnerize
That cloud, for instance?

    OLD RECTORY   Well, they'd be far back,
Such trials, if I made them, in the stack.
Clouds, lovely – ay: but probing them to find
Reality, what shall I find? *Le silence
Éternel de ces espaces infinis
M'effraie.* For, tell me, how did Turner cope
With life-as-creed? *The Fallacies of Hope.*
Interior at Petworth's not aligned
To the interior life. My moon would be
A Palmer moon, and visionary throng
Homing through Arcady from evensong;
Or Rembrandt's, dimmed by angels.

    RALPH   Scan the sky
With the eye's mind: a vast *in vacuo*
Of light-years to the nth. With the mind's eye

And, as to Shakespeare's gaze, the moon Peace ho!
Sleeps with Endymion. I don't equate
Latmos with Bethlehem, but merely state
The human psyche has observatories
Observatories know nothing of . . . Luke, please –
It is no chuckling matter.

*While talking the three hermits have left the terrace,
and move towards the church and its trees.*

DIRK   Memory,
You said just now, has markers, and for me
To-night itself will be one, and include
The cluster yonder we're about to reach
Of sycamore and sandstone, tower and tree
Immersed in moonlight, stance of masonry
Distinct beside the shadowy amplitude.

RALPH
Nocturnal red again.

DIRK   But in this case
The silver it's subdued to is the bleach
Of living lichen, in affinity
Itself with moonlight.

RALPH   That's no lichen-patch
Though, in the corner, by the buttress base,
Like a perched owl, but huger – in this light
Hard to make out – half tawny and half white.

DIRK   A piebald owl!

RALPH   Even if it doesn't match
Your lichen, Dirk, at least it's living – why,
It ambulates towards us . . . Malachi!

With Jerome beard and torso summer-buff.

OLD RECTORY
Telesperance! It's worked again all right.
I hoped he'd come if I hoped hard enough.

DIRK
Monksilver! named for such a tryst and night.

SCENE II

*As he reaches the nave of the church, Old Rectory
calls back to the lingering Dirk, who follows in almost
immediately.*

OLD RECTORY
Dirk, leave the open moonlight and rejoin
It walled in here, windowed across this dim
Interior. Chiaroscuro, eh?
(We mentioned Rembrandt – it might be by him).
If churchyard trees darken one aisle by day,
By night . . . Yet on the moonward side, the screen
Glistens and glimmers: glistens where its sheen
Catches the lustre; glimmers where the dust
Has whitened on its cornice, as it must
So far above my reach.

DIRK   Yes, even from here
Its sombre wood has highlights, boss and coign;
And we can see you've kept the chancel clear,
And one lamp lit.

RALPH   While round us in the gloom

Of your nave-atelier, all stack and pile,
The jumble – judging from the pews and aisle
We *can* see – more suggests an auction-room
Before the sale.

OLD RECTORY
                        And pulpit auctioneer?

DIRK
Or is it more like one of those remote
Italian churches, which, in the last war
(Almost remote itself) was stuffed to store
Art-treasures, masterpieces on the run
From some great Gallery, out of bomb's way;
Virgins and Venuses, dumped there to stay
For the duration, then whisked home again
And walled for worship, once more to sustain
Stare after millionth stare?

OLD RECTORY   How unlike these
Here dumped around you – when *they* leave the floor
It won't be for the wall: in twos or threes
Trundled away, I hope unglanced at.

RALPH   Luke,
This nave looks large; what do you do for light?

OLD RECTORY
Candles, old candles. By a lucky fluke
Some rector – I don't work here much at night –
Had candle-holders fitted on the pews,
Hand-wrought – no doubt there was a local smith.
Tallow-dips, too; he'd stocked a useful pile
Down in his cellar.

RALPH   These are all you use?

85

OLD RECTORY
Not quite. I have experimented with
Links, torches, flambeaux – call them what you will –
That flare across, not up – the usual style
In Muscovy (if that's no Hakluyt myth).
While as for flint and tinder, you've that skill
No less than I. Let's strike up. Dirk, the door . . .

*A light is struck, candles are lit down the pews and
the nave is illuminated.*

DIRK
Good Heavens, Luke, you've frescoed half the church.
No one at least could trundle these away.

OLD RECTORY
No need for trundling. Don't you see that smirch
Up there?

DIRK   Damp!

OLD RECTORY Damp, the wall mark of decay.
But come, I'll find these markers. While I search,
Do you set up the easel. For display
Let's use the largest – once a blackboard's perch.

*He moves across to sort out his pictures from a pile,
while the others go to fetch an easel. The one they select
gives rise to uncertainty, and Ralph goes across to
consult Old Rectory, who listens, puzzled.*

OLD RECTORY
No weather stains, or tell-tale splash of turd?
My dear Ralph, what I said was 'board' not 'bird'.

86

SCENE III

*The easel is set up between the pews and the screen,
and the three hermits cluster round it ; Malachi
tending to remain a little in the background.*

RALPH
So this is your first marker; not a work
That I should have expected as the first,
Being so apocalyptic.

OLD RECTORY   Not at all,
Since what the seraphs in the picture sound
Is the First Trump, not Last. Breughel, *The Fall
Of Rebel Angels.* D'you remember, Dirk,
That time in Brussels once when we went round
The Musée des Beaux Arts ? (Is Brussels still
Lived in, I wonder ?)

DIRK   Yes, and can recall
The picture, too; and how disturbing seemed
Its variation on the subject themed
By Milton. Could (I thought) this disarray
Of grotesque hybrids, this Discellany
Of monstrous and mutated composites
As it conglomerated the abyss
In flabbergasted metamorphosis
And welter-skelter – could this symbolize
The overthrow of evil in a mould
So unlike Satan, Moloch, Belial;
Or even that demonic posse which

Dante found names for, Rubicant', Cagnazzo
Gaffing the sinners in the boiling pitch?
But these concoctions...? Look, here, doing the splits,
A four-legged belly, amphisboena-wise.
And in the hullabrouhahaballoo
Gobbledegooks, flotzombies, orts with eyes;
A bolsturd rump-frump with a saurian maw.
Or this bizarre loblolly, look; or this:
Wig with a wam, frilled by a collaring
Of butterfly wing and wing;
Its globose torso tapered through a ring
Into a scaly stamen with a sting.

RALPH
Tohu he's called and Bohu.

DIRK   Here, indeed,
Anything gohues.

OLD RECTORY Not quite anything.
For though old Breughel's freak-for-all implies
Evil's divisiveness, antipathy
To pattern, desolating appetite
For entropy, preoccupation with
Disruption, discord, disaffection ...

DIRK   Dis,
In fact ...

OLD RECTORY
            yet, as you see, he typifies
The rebel followers of anti-Mind
Not as amorphous phantoms, but a rout
Of miscreations with a nightmare kind
Of sincoherence. Shapelessness defined

88

By random shape, as in a skyline sprout
Of unrelated tower-blocks.

    RALPH   So this brood
Of breakaways is fittingly subdued
By those who broke not, now their opposites
In guise and glory, willing the supreme
Ascendancy of holiness and wholeness.
Above the flounder of that zany swarm
How paramount their pattern, as they wheel
And wing in angel splendour; even the flow
And undulating curve of Michael's cloak
In contrast, like a contour of Welsh hills
Skirting some belch-arena's murk of mills.

    DIRK
It's almost possible to hear the din,
Sin's shindy – and that cosmic cry of 'Woe
To earth's inhabitants' – as down they go
With the cacophony of overthrow
To take poor Adam over.

    OLD RECTORY   Adam, true;
And all men since. And as I mused in paint
To symbolize that sequel as it grew
To its great climax in the world we knew
And fled from, what could I have found more apt
Than this strange vision of the primal taint
In heaven? So easy was it to adapt
Its disarray to ours, its plunging crew
To our progressive one; as fantasy
Without the least sense of anomaly
Would substitute for its *diablerie*

Jasjoycejabber, freaktures picasscalene
Tender as triangles, teenterrorists,
Genesjogglers, Godsgone clerics, mythoclasts,
Factotums of the great Fact-totem, all
Perdition's brinkmen; for scenario,
Lost Angeles, exEdenly choke-a-block
With traffic, a monstrocity.

DIRK   Out there,
Is all this starting up again, d'you think?

OLD RECTORY
The evidence suggests it may be so:
My interviewers – who, instead of showing
Symptoms of *metanoia*, seemed to me
Like ghosts returning from the *status quo*
To warn us. If that trio – there's no knowing –
Were typical out-therians, you'll see
Why this was my first marker, and agree
We needed its reminder, as we go
Back to a world astray, of what the breach
Was like, and of the cure we'll have to preach.

SCENE IV

*Old Rectory removes his first picture and replaces it
with a smaller one.*

MALACHI MONKSILVER
You raise an issue, Luke. If, as you say,
This allegory of egogerish sin
May still be relevant – as well it may –

90

To what revives out there, then why move in
Merely to re-encounter all that made
Us hermits? Better surely bide at home
Now we've been found, and voice the wilderness
To further visitants.

    OLD RECTORY   If you're dismayed
By my first marker, here's the second, which
Is no less apt, evoking in decay
That world whose bread-and-circus breakaway
Prefigured ours.

    RALPH   I guessed it would be Rome.

    DIRK
Breughel to Piranesi; quite a switch.
Sky at both corners; all the rest made dark
By arches; three colossal spans athwart
The whole scene, bridge-like. How the nearest arc
Enlarges its concavity of gloom
Above us; once the ceiling in a room
Of a huge palace, Nero's Golden House.
And golden still across each spacious court
Enormous slants of sunlight where goats browse
And to each pastoral apartment give
A rural air, that makes the whole arcade
Arcadian. And how diminutive
Men too, and even horses seem, as if
The blocks they carted, tumbled frieze or plinth,
Were from a quarry, and that wall its cliff.

    RALPH
And with its verdure looking like one, too;
And shrubs along its upper edge, the sort

Of airy shelf where Shelley might have strayed
And found, if not as in the labyrinth
Of Caracalla, actual copse and glade,
At least a poet's perch, with rural shade
Above, and Rome beneath him.

OLD RECTORY   Shelley, true.
[*half aside*] I had forgotten Shelley.

DIRK   What a freak
Of far-fetched prophecy to Horace (say)
It would have seemed, that a patrician bard
From Thule's fog would one day study Greek
Above a grassy Forum.

OLD RECTORY   If so hard
For him to have accepted (here forget
Shelley's intrusion) how much harder yet
Had someone put it up to him, by way
Of oracle-conjecture, that a Jew,
Plebeian, dubiously parented
And put to death obscurely, with a creed
Of love and sacrifice would overset
Not just some minor province, but the sway
Of absolute Rome itself, and supersede
Triumphal arches, pedimented aisles,
Caesar and Senate.

RALPH   With urbane dismay,
Si fractus orbis Horace quotes and smiles.

OLD RECTORY
Yet *ferient ruinae* – as we view.
Such vestiges as these prestige the past
All the world over – Wiltshire or Peru,

Angkor or Karnak – Syrian or Greek –
But these are singular, perhaps unique,
Not in the stretch and structure of their vast
Canopy, but one adjunct – Malachi
Come closer – so obscure you'll have to pry
To find it. Scan the sky there, through that wide
Tier of six apertures, each bay so big
The lofty wall-end of that church outside
Blocks only two, and leaves above its line
Of roof a gap of light, and there, enskied –
There, where I'm pointing – what might seem a twig
Crossed by a twig. How inconspicuous
In Piranesi's peephole; yet the sign
And symbol of a faith in the divine
Transcending the majestic wear and tear
Of Rome around it. And if Rome's decline
Saw faith's ascension, from our moral slide
So similar, why may it not – by us
Evangelized – why may it not out there
Fulfil once more men's yearning for the whole
And holy, archetypal in the soul?

RALPH
So Jung affirmed.

MALACHI   But Jung affirmed as well
The presence of the shadow; and how dark
It was for us: the sombre menace-blot
Of Bomb and Belsen, and corrupting spell
Of our inventions. If those doomsday powers
Rome knew not, yet without them touched a mark
Of such deep degradation that the best
Alone, Christ's coming, could redeem it, what
Climacteric awaits a world like ours

Far deeper sunk? Who has not sometimes guessed:
Apocalypse?

DIRK   Yet can we also see
The Plague as such, its vast calamity
Like a suspended sentence, a last chance
For lives to change allegiance; not to made
Now, but to Maker.

MALACHI   Ay: though we can't tell –
Yet – if they're taking it.

RALPH   Or – yet – if aid
From us will help to put them on the way
Back to Reality; where even two
Or three are gathered, so that, passing through
Things temporal, they finally lose not
The things eternal. And, for those who do,
What matters world-duration; distant, near,
Millennia or minutes, the Great Year
Of Plato, or next week?

DIRK   Surely the need
Is crucial, and if so, our mission's clear.

OLD RECTORY
Crucial, crux, Cross – the word is apt indeed.
When next we view, it will be to revere.

SCENE V

Old Rectory removes his rendering of Piranesi,
and returns it to a stack by the wall; while
the others dismantle the easel, before rejoining him in
the centre aisle.

RALPH
So we exchange the easel for the wall,
And nave for chancel. Wouldn't it be best
To fire these cressets, Luke, and amplify
The candleshine, if we're to see at all
Up by the altar?

OLD RECTORY   I'm not sure the flare
Will do much for my markers – still, let's try
What the effect is.

He takes a candle from its socket, and kindles
the torches down each side of the nave.

DIRK   In the roof up there
At least it has one – did you see that waft
Of startled white – as soundless and as soft
As the gliding of a snowflake?

OLD RECTORY   From its nest
We've scared my owl to find its way out where
The ivy finds one in.

DIRK   And what a scare
It must have had, poor resident, recessed

In darkness, when it saw – so near its perch –
Your frescoed walls, unshadowed by the glare,
Like pictured perpendiculars emerge.

RALPH
Pictured indeed. You told us of your quest
And mahlstick meditation. But to me
More like an act of worship seems this church,
Painted *ad gloriam dei ;* less a search
Than celebration.

OLD RECTORY
    [*doubtfully*] Well . . .

DIRK   Or was your plan
To have a terrace here, where you could scan
This inner sky, and view mythology's
Equivalent to the great gallery
Of clouds you gazed at in the outer one ?
Episodes from the Bible's said-and-done
That took for granted the adjacency
Of heaven.

*Here Old Rectory sits down at the end of a
pew, and the others do the same around him,
in a cluster, each side of the aisle.*

OLD RECTORY
            And how supreme – from Genesis
To Judgement – a mythology it is.
Still is – and still again, as in times gone,
Could interfuse a sense of the divine
Into the everyday of Everyman.
(Even the Wife of Bath rode to a shrine.)

RALPH

And what a shrine! So medieval man
Marshalled his creativity, to build
With all his mind, and carve with all his heart,
And glaze with all his soul. Yet not just there,
Cathedral-awed, but outside, on all sides,
He'd be reminded of his destiny,
And made aware, by symbols tangible,
He was in touch with life intangible.
A devil-knocker, say, or market cross,
Or Pilgrims' Inn, niched with its patron saint;
Flight into Egypt on a coffer lid;
Jericho shouted down in tapestry;
Or Caleb, with his outsize bunch of grapes
Pole-slung, a two-man load in alabaster;
Or seraph winged above a feaster's salt,
Or the apostle spoon he took it with.

MALACHI

Men loved to decorate. But let's admit
Misericords had mermaids. Kilpeck's trolls
And woodwos hardly followed Holy Writ.

DIRK

Nor did the bear with bagpipes which a monk
Across the margin of a breviary
Wheeled in a barrow. But the book itself –
Grimani, Sforza, Rohan, *Très Riches Heures* –
I can't remember which – why, every page
Seemed half in Heaven – not just for the colour,
Illumination – but the myth portrayed,
Illuminatio; portrayed as if
It happened round the corner, yesterday.

97

Jerusalem is Paris; Bethlehem
Might be the Windrush valley, Burford-spired;
Christ's hauled to Herod through the streets of Bruges.
A world that flowered to God as rose to sun,
And with a rose's splendour. Here you have it,
Between a missal's covers – Christendom.

RALPH
Whole, too, as well as holy. Not alone
Gorgeous Epiphany or darkened leaf
Of Crucifixion, but the workaday
Months' Occupations (even their calendar
Cosmos-connected through the zodiac).
How vividly those pages – this from one,
That from another volume – I recall,
Like Georgics with a background of St George:
Vine-pruning in white-castled Burgundy;
Or shearing session by a Flemish moat;
Or perched December windmill, snowy sails
Like silver trellises; or festal bevy,
Wardrobed, let's say, in cloth-of-paradise,
On May's first morning.
                                    Oh yes, sin abounded,
Plague, famine, serfdom, rapine, massacre
(Those lick-lip faces round the fainting Christ
Were local, too). And yet, if virtue veered,
Faith was a constant; and the creature man,
Myth-linked to his Creator, hence derived
Through certainty of supernatural order
His order, and eternal reference.

OLD RECTORY
Imagine the equivalent, to-day's

(Pre-plague, so more precisely – yesterday's)
Album of progress open-paged before us:
Goods in, God out and order out, and chase
For orders in; the urban workday there
Slumdrum and wheel-base; in the countryside
(In the unpeace of the ex-countryside)
The tractor's idyll and the dawnsaw chorus.
A world out for itself, impose, deface.
A scientific world, cock-lensed in space,
So that its farthest far and widest wide
Is an interminable everywhere
Of matter, daunting vision, dumbing prayer,
So *cor in se curvatus* and to grace
Impervious. But for those two twigs crossed,
A world, as once before, literal and lost
Their symbol, upright still, as in that chink
Of ruined Rome, beyond material fact
Sustains the sense of myth, so keeps the link
Between us and Reality intact.

MALACHI
Myth? Myth is what I call a fallen word.
Preach it, you'll find the meaning that's inferred
Is not your meaning, but the opposite.
Why, you yourself just now made use of it –
No Hakluyt myth – in that sense.

OLD RECTORY   Ay, indeed –
The torches. So we'll have to clarify
And re-instate it. There's no synonym
For myth. 'Mere myth'? Then how about, say I,
Mere fact? Since even nursery tales can yield
Truth deeper than mere fact. In Homer's sky

99

Men feared the Thunderer as thunder's cause,
And worshipped. Yet from city, shore and field
The smoke of sacrifice, the temple hymn
Rose not in mere delusion, but revealed
The soul's response, its archetypal need
For the transcendent sacred, and a creed
With mystery's involvement, wonder's, awe's;
Hence Paestum, Parthenon. Hence, too, my third
Marker, which illustrates it, and comes pat
To fetch us to our feet again, who've sat
Too long in this pew-session. It's as well
The light's uncertain, since my rendering's
Uncertain too.

    DIRK   As well there is no glazing
To glint reflections – how they used to mar
Old Masters. So you've turned to the Baroque
And Rubens – Adoration of the Kings.
A stable – and a group of figures gazing;
And gazing up ourselves to check its source
Of light – a swag of thatch just blocks it out,
Moon or miraculous star, we're left in doubt –
We don't anticipate – shock follows shock –
The exquisite Corinthian shaft that shores
A fringe; still less, those supercilious
Intruding camels, lofty heads aloof;
And, high up on their humps, a pair of brown
And brawny tribesmen, perched close to the roof
But from the sky outside it craning down,
Engrossed.

    RALPH   Intrusion so spectacular
Might here distract, did not the figures under

Assert themselves in such a sovereignty
Of varied presence; a fixed gaze of wonder
All that they have in common. Ours is free
To come to rest on each arrested glance;
That horseman's, say, still reining in the prance
Of his checked charger to stare down across
The midriff of a burly Prester John:
The posture of a potentate, sash, toque
And ruby – how it glows, that gorgeous boss,
In spite of the voluminous scarlet cloak
Worn by his whitebeard neighbour, royal sage,
Plato's philosopher-king, who's holding up,
And waiting to present, a golden cup;
While – his presented – kneeling with his page,
The foremost of them – silked like Solomon,
But with the Psalmist's look of tender zest
And worship – gazes on creation's guest;
Their treasure's treasure, quarry of their quest.

OLD RECTORY
And mine. Whether it happened in mere fact,
It happened in this picture; on this floor
Happened to me, and taught me through the act
Of painting adoration to adore.

MALACHI
True, true. But wise men now come from the West,
With actual-factual attitudes. For them
Myth, dream and mystical experience
Are so much wish-fulfilment; and their test
Is: did those camels come to Bethlehem
Or did they not?

RALPH   Who knows?

MALACHI   So, if the sense
Of myth is still to keep, as you suggest,
The heavenly option open, and the link
Intact, our only life-line – in this case
Our otherlife-line – so we do not sink
In the interminable everywhere
Of matter – myth itself must have a base
In fact; a date, that is, in history.
If not, dismissable as fantasy.

OLD RECTORY
A date so manifest that its event
Initiated a new calendar.
For our Olympus is the Mount of Olives.
Prometheus was judged by Pontius Pilate,
A name well-known to the Establishment,
And entry of some length in Rome's *Quis't Quis*.
Coal in a brazier warmed Peter's hands.
Below the naked body soldiers diced,
Winner take all, one throw, the perks of Christ.
Christ, very myth and very man; the man
Needful – how else implant the myth in time?
The myth affirming, as no history can,
Life's purport and affinity sublime.

SCENE VI

Still conversing, the hermits pause at the entrance to the chancel, as they prepare to enter through the screen to the altar.

RALPH
Life's purport – how precariously preserved
By one sole people; first a tiny tribe,
Then a small nation monstrously be-neighboured
By militarism and growth idolatry,
Assyrian bull, pyramid super-power;
And yet in voice and inspiration still
Moses, Isaiah and the Psalms live on;
Tiglath-pileser and Sennacherib,
Merodach-baladan, Belshazzar gone.
So Christ preserved it through the gloat and bloat
Of Rome, and our deformed enormities,
Nuclear, New York and Gulag. At what cost
Preserved it, when on Calvary were crossed
Those two twigs.

OLD RECTORY So a last reminding gaze
At my last marker – yonder – not the walled
And frescoed Crucifixion – but you'll see
A curtained panel in the candlespace
Upon the altar, where I've tried to trace
Those features stained upon the Holy Shroud.
How many times the likeness of that face
Has been endeavoured – Rembrandt, Grunewald,
Raphael, da Vinci – the Last Supper, bowed

Upon the Cross, the gaze of risen glory –
But never to convince us – till this smear
Of sweat on linen – and how strange its story –
Reveals to us beyond expectancy
The face that we expect; serene, august,
Majestic rectitude, compassion just,
Death-mask of perfect life – of all things here
That most I would remember . . .

*Here Old Rectory pauses, interrupted by a commotion
that seems to come from the porch outside.*

MALACHI   What's that din,
That banging on the door? And voices called.

VOICES [*from the porch*]
Rector, we want our second interview.

The four gaze at each other in questioning astonishment.

OLD RECTORY
My interviewers! I've misgauged the dose,
And they've recovered; followed, I suppose,
The light up here.

DIRK   It's side-effects, no doubt,
Makes them sound tipsy.

MALACHI   Why don't they come in?

DIRK I locked the door.

MALACHI   Admit or not admit?
Luke, it's your sanctum; tell us what to do.

VOICES [*in chorus*]
You fossick me, I torquemada you.

OLD RECTORY
Admit them, here, now? – not on any score
Will I admit them. There's an outside door
Leads from the vestry – let's make use of it,
And leave them on their own to brawl and shout.

RALPH
Scarper? They'll guess we mean to when we dout
The torches. How demeaning, to be tracked
Among the graves; detected in the fact
As fugitives.

OLD RECTORY Then what do you suggest?

MALACHI
Leave it to me, my friends. You may have guessed
I shan't be joining you in any case.
Apocalypse, Parousia is due
Shortly, I think – why emigrate to face
Finality? So I can take your place,
And grant your friends their second interview.

OLD RECTORY
What can we say to that? How can we part
In such a scramble?

MALACHI   Best, before they start
Breaking the glass. [*Raising his voice*] All right,
I'm coming round.
[*Quietly*] Off – lock the door behind you – not a sound.

*They hesitate; but he ushers them towards the vestry.
They vanish, with gestures of farewell; and he walks
slowly down the nave towards the main door.*

SCENE VII

Outside the three fugitives reach a turn in the path where
they can just get a last view of the church ; and they
pause to take it.

DIRK

The moon casts shadows still; but from the brink
Of the horizon, look, a tinge of day.
So on the tower the silver seems to shrink,
Pervaded by a glimmer of first grey.
How reticent it looks, serene and grave.
I wonder what's going on within the nave.

RALPH

Does not the daybreak aptly symbolize
Lifebreak for us ? On that first Easter morn
Did those who reached the sepulchre surmise
Or sense that more than day had been re-born,
More than sun risen ? Or when Mary heard
The greeting in the garden, the first word
Spoken by risen life on earth ?

OLD RECTORY   For me . . .

DIRK

By risen life. Barren as Calvary
And bleak with thorns the cactus – then, behold,
From its barbed rind new growth, a sudden surge
Exploding into splendour, pale and gold;
Consummate contrast! How can such emerge
From such ? – yet this is but a plant.

OLD RECTORY   For me
More like the dawn of Peter's cock-crow, this.
Failure to meet a crisis, craven flight –
Went ever start of mission more amiss?
How cope with many if I can't with three?

   RALPH
Perhaps a timely warning, if we see
Ourselves as heading movements, spreading light,
When we may merely join a new St Paul
As humble followers, and cast our mite
In his grand treasury – our best so done.
Francis de Sales said: Imitate a child
With one hand in its Father's, as with one
It stoops to gather garden fruits or wild.
So, if the crop we find is sparse or thick,
Success or failure, impact great or small,
Let us still act as hermits and recall
(To lack of men's response long reconciled)
Non nobis Domine, for whom we pick.